ALISTAIR FINDLAY is the author of *Shale Voices*, a social history of the shale oil communities of West Lothian, first published by Luath Press in 1999, with a second edition due in 2007 containing 'teaching notes' for use in schools. His two poetry collections are also published by Luath, *Sex, Death and Football* (2003) and *The Love Songs of John Knox* (2006). He has a Masters Degree in Modern Poetry in English from Stirling University. A Social Work Manager for West Lothian Council until August 2007, he was awarded a Writer's Bursary by the Scottish Arts Council to produce a

PHOTO: BOB WALLACE

The editor, on the right, in his playing days.

third collection of poems on social workers – *Dancing With Big Eunice* – and to edit an anthology of Scottish Marxist poetry – *Lenin's Gramophone*. Between 1965–1968, he was a part-time provisional professional footballer with Hibernian FC, during which time he never got the ball off Peter Marinello once, or beat George McNeill in a sprint.

D0293501

100 FAVOURITE SCOTTISH FOOTBALL POEMS

EDITED BY ALISTAIR FINDLAY

Luath Press Limited

EDINBURGH

www.luath.co.uk

First published 2007

ISBN (10): 1-906307-03-2
ISBN (13): 978-1-906307-03-5

The publishers acknowledge the support of

 Scottish **Arts** Council

towards the publication of this volume.

The paper used in this book is recyclable. It is made from low-chlorine
pulps produced in a low-emission manner from renewable forests.

Printed and bound by
Creative Print and Design, Wales

Typeset in ITC Charter and Gill Sans by
3btype.com

for
Angus Calder, Big Vince Halpin, Joseph

CONTENTS

Acknowledgements

Foreword by Tony Higgins

Introduction

ACKNOWLEDGEMENTS

Thanks to the Scottish Arts Council for funding towards this book.

Thanks to David Purdie for unearthing, and reciting from memory, the anonymous poem 'Scottish League Cup Final, 1959 Hearts 2 – Third Lanark 1' which was printed in the Programme of that Final.

Thanks to the Scottish Poetry Library staff for their help and resources.

Thanks to Angus Calder who made this book seem possible and worth doing.

Thanks to Andrew Philip for commenting on the book in draft.

Our thanks are also due to the authors, publishers and estates who have generously given permission to reproduce poems:

James Aitchison, 'The Half-Time Dancer' from *Second Nature* (Mercat Press,1990), reproduced courtesy of the author; Lilian Anderson, 'The Blues', reproduced courtesy of the author; D. M. Black, 'The Visitor' from *Collected Poems 1964–87*, (Polygon, 1991), reproduced courtesy of Polygon, an imprint of Birlinn Ltd, www.birlinn.co.uk; Alan Bold, 'Andy Gray' from *Scotland, Yes: World Cup Football Poems* (Paul Harris Publishing, 1978) and the extract 'Jimmy Johnstone' from 'Football Triptych' from *A Pint of Bitter* (The Hogarth Press, 1971), reproduced courtesy of Alice Bold (copyright Alan Bold to Alice Bold); George Bruce, 'Boys: In a Crowd' from *Today Tomorrow, The Collected Poems of George Bruce, 1933–2000* (Polygon, 2001), reproduced courtesy of Polygon, an imprint of Birlinn Ltd, www.birlinn.co.uk; Tom Bryan, 'Pittodrie Winter, 4.45pm' from *North East Passage* (Scottish Cultural Press, 1996), reproduced courtesy of Scottish Cultural Press, www.scottishbooks.com; John Burnside, 'Euro 96: A Fan's Farewell' reproduced courtesy of the author; Ron Butlin, 'Argentina, 1978' from *Without a Backward Glance: New and Selected Poems* (Barzan Publishing, 2005), reproduced courtesy of the author; Angus Calder, 'I. M. Davie Cooper, d. March 95' from *Walking in Waikato* (Diehard, 1997), reproduced courtesy of the author; Angus Peter Campbell, 'The Best Goal I Ever Scored' from *The Greatest Gift* (Fountain Publishing, 1992) and 'St Mirren 3 Aberdeen 1' from *One Road* (Fountain Publishing, 1994), reproduced courtesy of the author; Stewart Conn, 'The Barber-Surgeons to King James IV' from *Ghosts at Cockcrow* (Bloodaxe, 2005), reproduced courtesy of Bloodaxe Books; Robert Crawford, 'Identity League' from *The Tip of My Tongue* (Jonathan Cape, 2003), reprinted by permission of The Random House Group Ltd; Iain

Crichton Smith, extract from 'Oban 1955–1982' from *Collected Poems* (Carcanet, 1995), reproduced courtesy of Carcanet Press Limited; Julia Darling, 'World Cup Summer', from *Sauces, The Poetry Virgins* (Bloodaxe, 1994), reproduced courtesy of Bev Robinson; Mike Dillon, 'The Big Yin' from *Football: Pure Poetry* (Creative Energy Publications, 1999), reproduced courtesy of the author; Douglas Dunn, 'The Sportsmen' from *Selected Poems* (Faber & Faber, 1986), reproduced courtesy of Faber & Faber; G. F. Dutton, 'Penalty' from *The Bare Abundance* (Bloodaxe, 2002), reproduced courtesy of Bloodaxe Books; Matthew Fitt, 'Jim Leighton' from *Kate O'Shanter's Tale and Other Poems* (Luath, 2003), reproduced courtesy of Luath Press Ltd; Bashabi Fraser, 'Do' Care' from *Tartan and Turban* (Luath, 2004), reproduced courtesy of Luath Press Ltd; Raymond Friel, 'May 1967' from *Seeing the River* (Polygon, 1995), reproduced courtesy of the author; Robert Garioch, 'Fi'baw in the Street' from *Robert Garioch: Collected Poems* (Polygon, 2004), reproduced courtesy of Polygon, an imprint of Birlinn Ltd, www.birlinn.co.uk; Duncan Glen, 'Fitbaaer' from *Feres* (Akros Publications, 1971) and 'John Kennedy, steelworker, 1939–1975' from *Collected Poems 1965–2005* (Akros Publications, 2006), reproduced courtesy of the author; Sydney Goodsir Smith, from 'Kynd Kittock's Land' from *Collected Poems* (Calder Publications, 1975), reproduced courtesy of Calder Publications Ltd; Andrew Greig, 'The Oldest Game' from *Men on Ice* (Canongate, 1977), reproduced courtesy of the author; George Gunn, 'Twisted Knee' from *Sting* (Chapman, 1991), reproduced courtesy of Chapman; Mike Harding, 'Daddy Edgar's pools' from *Daddy Edgar's Pools* (Peterloo Poets, 1992), reproduced courtesy of the author; W. N. Herbert, 'Song of the Sub-Welshian' from *Bad Shaman Blues* (Bloodaxe, 2006), reproduced courtesy of Bloodaxe Books; William Hershaw, 'Johnny Thompson' from *Dream State* (Polygon, 2004), reproduced courtesy of the author; Billy Hunter, 'Long Ago the Goalie's Fear' from *Look Back in Amber and Claret*, reproduced courtesy of the author; Robert Alan Jamieson, 'The Day that Britain Split', reproduced courtesy of the author; Jackie Kay, 'Girl Footballer' from *The Frog Who Dreamed She Was An Opera Singer* (Bloomsbury, 1998), reproduced courtesy of Bloomsbury; Jim Kay, 'Directions' from *A Bitia Tarzan Film*, reproduced courtesy of the author; Tom Leonard, 'Unrelated Incidents (4)', 'The Good Thief' and 'Crack' from *Intimate Voices: Selected Works 1965–1983* (Vintage, 1995), and from 'situations theoretical and contemporary' and '4 football haiku' from *Access to the Silence: poems 1984–2004* (Galloping Dog Press, 1986), reproduced courtesy of the author; Maurice Lindsay, 'After the Game', reproduced courtesy of the author; Liz Lochhead, 'Men Monologue: Annemarie' from *True Confessions and New Clichés* (Polygon, 1985), reproduced courtesy of

Polygon, an imprint of Birlinn Ltd, www.birlinn.co.uk; Norman MacCaig, 'Composers of music' from *Collected Poems* (Chatto & Windus, 1988), reproduced courtesy of Birlinn Ltd, www.birlinn.co.uk; Hugh MacDiarmid, 'Glasgow, 1960' from *Complete Poems* (Carcanet, 1993), reproduced courtesy of Carcanet Press Ltd; George MacKay Brown, 'January the Twenty-Fifth' from *Northern Lights: A Poet's Sources* (John Murray, 1999), reproduced courtesy of John Murray (Publishers) Limited; Colin MacKinnon, 'Penalty: In memoriam of Jock Stein' from *An Tuil, Anthology of 20th Century Scottish Gaelic Verse* (Polygon, 1999), reproduced courtesy of Polygon, an imprint of Birlinn Ltd, www.birlinn.co.uk; Parry Maguire, 'Alex Young', 'Billy Bremner', 'Dennis Law' and 'The Entry of Shankley to Liverpool' from *Beautiful Game*, reproduced courtesy of the author; Brian McCabe, 'Ball' from *Body Parts* (Canongate, 1999), reproduced courtesy of Canongate Books; John McCaughie, 'The Scottish Junior Cup Final' from *Football: Pure Poetry 2* (Creative Energy Publications, 2002), reproduced courtesy of the author; Andrew McGeever, 'Stairway', reproduced courtesy of the author; Tom McGrath, 'there was that time charlie tully' from *Mungo's Tongues: Glasgow poems 1630–1990* (Mainstream, 1993), reproduced courtesy of the author; William McIlvanney, 'What the Crowd Said' from *In Through the Head* (Mainstream, 1988), reproduced courtesy of the author; Hugh McMillan, 'Anglophobia' from *Tramontana* (Dog & Bone Press, 1990), reproduced courtesy of the author; Ian McMillan, 'Somewhere on the South China Sea in 1938', reproduced courtesy of the author; Adrian Mitchell, 'Golo, the Gloomy Goalkeeper' from *Blue Coffee Poems 1985–1996* (Bloodaxe, 1997), reproduced courtesy of Peters, Fraser and Dunlop; Edwin Morgan, 'The Divan (86)' from *Collected Poems 1949–1987* (Carcanet, 1996), reproduced courtesy of Carcanet Press Limited; Ken Morrice, 'Match of the Day' from *Talking of Michaelangelo* (Scottish Cultural Press, 1996), reproduced courtesy of Scottish Cultural Press, www.scottishbooks.com; Stephen Mulrine, 'The Coming of the Wee Malkies', reproduced courtesy of the author; William Neill, 'Two Skills' from *Just Sonnets* (Burnside Press, 1996), reproduced courtesy of the author; Liz Niven, 'Edwin Muir's Furst Fitba' from *Stravaigin* (Luath, 2006), reproduced courtesy of Luath Press Ltd; Sean O'Brien, 'Football! Football! Football!' from *Cousin Coat: Selected Poems 1976–2001* (© Sean O'Brien, 2002), reproduced courtesy of Pan Macmillan, London; Dennis O'Donnell, 'Fid. Def.' from *Two Clocks Ticking* (Curly Snake Publishing, 1997), reproduced courtesy of the author; Donny O'Rourke, 'Robbie' from *Dream State: The New Scottish Poets* (Polygon, 2002), reproduced courtesy of Polygon, an imprint of Birlinn Ltd, www.birlinn.co.uk; Janet Paisley, 'James: Fitba Daft' from *Ye Cannae Win* (Chapman, 2002), reproduced courtesy of Chapman;

Don Paterson, 'Nil Nil' from *Nil Nil* (Faber & Faber, 1993), reproduced courtesy of Faber & Faber; Tom Pow, 'The Football' from *Landscapes and Legacies* (iynx, 2003), reproduced courtesy of the author; James T. R. Ritchie, 'Herts' from *A Cinema of Days* (The Albyn Press, 1960), reproduced courtesy of Dr Margaret Longstaff; James Robertson, 'Glasgow 2015' from *Sound Shadow* (Black & White Publishing, 1995), reproduced courtesy of Black & White Publishing; Derek Ross, 'First Gemme', reproduced courtesy of the author; Christopher Salvesen, 'Parish Football' from *A Nest of Singing Birds* (Fettes College, 1995), reproduced courtesy of the author; Stephen Scobie, 'Saturday Night', reproduced courtesy of the author; Alexander Scott, 'Scotch Soccer' from *Collected Poems: 1920–1990* (Mercat, 1990), reproduced courtesy of Mercat, an imprint of Birlinn Ltd, www.birlinn.co.uk; Ian Stephen, 'Echaler' from *Varying States of Grace* (Polygon, 1989), reproduced courtesy of Polygon, an imprint of Birlinn Ltd, www.birlinn.co.uk; Derick Thomson/Ruaraidh MacThòmais, 'Scotland v Argentine 2/6/79' from *Plundering the Harp, Collected Poems 1940–1980* (MacDonald Publishers, 1982), reproduced courtesy of the author; Raymond Vettese, 'Green Pairk Days' from *A Keen New Air* (The Saltire Society, 1995) and 'Jock Stein', reproduced courtesy of the author; Lorna Waite, 'Football Haikus' reproduced courtesy of the author; Sarah Wardle, 'In the Bill Nicholson Suite' from *Score*! (Bloodaxe, 2005), reproduced courtesy of Bloodaxe Books; Brian Whittingham, 'The Difficulties of Discipline on the Football Field' from *Swiss Watches & The Ballroom Dancer* (Taranus Books, 1996), reproduced courtesy of the author.

FOREWORD

I must admit when I was asked by Alistair Findlay to write a foreword for his Anthology I accepted with a sense of trepidation. 'Poetry in Motion' is hardly a term that misty eyed Hibs fans would remember me by, but how can you turn down a request from a fellow Hibee?

I derived immense enjoyment from reading the poems, it brought back many memories of some of the giants of football I was lucky to share the same field as – Bremner, Dalglish, Johnstone and Baxter to name but a few. The poems evoked many of the human emotions that football fans swear they experience; love, devotion, humour and tragedy, confirming football in Scottish society as one of our great cultural icons. The disparate language and composition of the poems reflects the diversity of opinion and dialect in different parts of Scotland and how they view our national game.

I was pleased to note a poem from Motherwell great Billy Hunter, who raises many questions about the quality of football today in comparison to the halcyon days of the 50s, 60s and 70s. Who said players' 'brains are in their feet'? Alistair I know by his own admission would never claim a place in 'football's hall of fame', but by bringing together this unique collection of poems he has ensured his place in the cultural history of our game.

Tony Higgins

TONY HIGGINS made 165 appearances and scored 41 goals for Hibernian FC over nine seasons, then joined Partick Thistle for two seasons, followed by two seasons at Morton. He then had a spell as player/coach at Stranraer before retiring in 1987. He then worked for the Scottish Professional Footballers Association in 1985, becoming its General Secretary, in which post he served until December 2006, when he joined Fifpro (Worldwide Players Union) with a special responsibility for Politics, Education and Discrimination issues.

INTRODUCTION

This anthology contains many of 20th century Scotland's best poets, drawn from well beyond the confines of its industrial central belt. A boy growing up in Orkney in the 1930s, George MacKay Brown exemplifies the social and cultural response of most Scots of his class, gender and generation to the game's drama and spectacle – whether island, rural, town or city bred:

> At night, in the bedroom George shared with his brothers, he invented imaginary teams and played them off against each other in his mind, throwing dice to decide the result of each game. In the early 30s, the first wireless sets had begun to arrive in Stromness. Very few families owned one and, for those who did, listening was plagued by what were called 'atmospherics': the volume rose and fell 'as though Henry Hall was playing from a raft somewhere in the mid-Atlantic'. For George, nevertheless, it seemed a magical experience to crouch over a neighbour's wireless on a Saturday afternoon listening to fragmentary murmurs from Hampden Park or Wembley. The Celtic footballers became, in his mind, figures invested with as much romance as the kings and queens of Scotland, and when, one day, he overheard a woman reading a newspaper to her father and learned that the great Celtic goalkeeper John Thomson had died after a collision in a match with Rangers, it seemed a tragedy as vivid as Fotheringhay or Flodden.[1]

In these poems, the literary imagination and popular culture meet, often to brilliant effect. Football – 'the thing itself' – is referred to either directly, as Ezra Pound advocated, or by metaphor: football as war, religion, socialism, homosexual love, mountain-climbing, music and misogyny. Enveloping all is the popular origin of 'the game' and its grip on 'the crowd' – really only another name for 'the people'. The 'voice' of 'the people', which has more often been heard in Scottish history and literature as a distant, throaty rumble,

[1] *George MacKay Brown: The Life*, Maggie Fergusson, John Murray, London, 2006, 34

in these pages, speaks for itself, and from within its own vast store of pent-up energy, amusement or rage.

The 'high culture' of poetry thus meets the 'low culture' of football, a contention which resides at the heart of Hugh MacDiarmid's 'anti-football' poem 'Glasgow, 1960', first published in the *London Mercury* in 1935. 'Glasgow, 1960' revolves round the poet's fantasy that in a socialist future 'the crowd' (the masses) would be flocking to the latest international poetry festival as though it were a Glasgow football match. Writing in the mid-1930s, the Bolshevik inspired MacDiarmid could indeed mischievously compare the 'philistine' culture – the 'kailyardism' – of a docile Scottish working-class to that of its revolutionary brethren in the Soviet Union – where poetry readings, chess-matches, ballet and the like had in reality attracted mass audiences, enough to fill even the largest football stadiums.

MacDiarmid's unreliable Marxism never did embrace 'the feck' (the ignorant Scots peasantry) or their traditional literature – balladry and folk-song – though this is not the case in respect of his trusted crony, Sydney Goodsir Smith, who catches the demotic vigour of Scotland's 'lower orders' marvellously well in 'Kynd Kittock's Land'. Goodsir Smith – who shared some of MacDiarmid's socialism but mostly his reverence for the literary Scots of the Old Makars and a bohemian outlook (bevvying with the literati in Embro's 'low-dives') – once cited his recreations as 'drinking and blethering', sentiments as dear to the Tartan Army as they no doubt were to Hugh MacDiarmid, Scotland's greatest, if also its most awkwardly critical, modern poet.

A poem by another friend of MacDiarmid, Norman MacCaig, who never actually wrote about football in his life, is included on the basis that the metonyms 'skidding', 'earth' and 'sponge-bag' in his 'Composers of music' conjure up, to this editor at least, the image of Jimmy Johnstone, flying down the wing. 'Composers of music' thus finds itself placed alongside Alan Bold's 'Jimmy Johnstone' which depicts 'Wee Jimmy' as the terracings best remember him, as remember him they do, and mourn his departure, and not simply from the football field. For 'death' features significantly in this volume too, of the famous, like Jock Stein and Davie Cooper, and, for some reason, goal-keepers, the tragic death of John Thomson eerily straddling both categories. These 'commemorative' poems have been placed alongside those which grieve Scotland's early exit from the World Cup in Argentina in 1978 – for a footballing nation surely another kind of 'passing'.

Other poems 'mourn' in more singular fashion: for the 66 lives lost 30 years ago when a stand collapsed at Ibrox stadium, for the 'loss' of childhood, for the memory of fathers or grandfathers, for an allegedly more 'innocent' past, for the absence of European football from Pittodrie. John White, the legendary 'Ghost of White Hart Lane', so-called even before his freak death, aged 27, struck by lightning while sheltering under a tree in 1964, is commemorated – without being specifically named – by Sarah Wardle in her poem, 'In the Bill Nicholson Suite'. Sarah was poet-in-residence for Tottenham Hotspur FC. John White was of course part of the famous Spurs 1960-61 Team that won the 'Double', which also included the magnificent Dave MacKay. It is in the august Anglo-Scots International company of Dave MacKay, Denis Law, Billy Bremner and Kenny Dalglish that the self-effacing John White belongs, and ought to be remembered, a spectral figure still, in the history of the modern game.

The variety of 'eras' and 'viewpoints' conjured up in these poems is extraordinary, as are the multiplicity of 'venues' and 'parks' over which their protagonists stride: a sloping Borders' field on a 1930s evening; a 1970s Glasgow ship-yard's tea-break tussle; a north-east fishing-town on a Saturday afternoon in the 1950s; a brutal, mindless, 'after the game' city-death in 1974. Such dramatic differences, and yet such overarching similarities, the outcome of a common but strongly var-iegated language and culture whose voices are unmistakably plebian, working-class, proletarian, and un-bourgeois. The range of languages and dialects employed is accordingly enormous – Gaelic, Lallans, Doric, central, urban and rural Scots, English – all crowding together inside the same small stadium. Scotland small! – as MacDiarmid once cried – though it seems this cry was heard, the one to the poets about giving full-reign to the Scots tongue. On the evidence of this anthology, that tongue is now clearly and unredeemably multi-voiced, polyglot and polyphonic.

The earliest poem on offer is from the Maitland Folio, written by 'anonymous' around 1580, and therefore 'The Bewteis of the Fute-ball' was almost certainly written by a woman. Another woman, or 'women' more like, is probably responsible for 'Donald Gorm's Lullaby', 1650, an anonymous Gaelic ballad, told in the voice of Donald's 'nurse'. Poems about football written by anyone prior to the 20th century are like poems written by women about football in the 20th century – few and far between. I have thus been able to include 15 poems by women poets. However, the anthology does end on something of a hopeful note by looking forward, with James Robertson in 'Glasgow 2015', to the year when Ibrox will make its first female signing. 'Glasgow 2015' in fact is an 'update' of Hugh MacDiarmid's 'Glasgow 1960' while Tom Leonard's 'situations theoretical and contemporary' takes a 'dig' at MacDiarmid's high-seriousness, a trait that could sometimes turn all too easily into high-cultural elitism. Tom Leonard's squib is a reminder, if any were needed, that literary exclusion – whether of women or of the natural speech of the Scottish lower orders – has only relatively recently been put into reverse – and verse! – not least through Leonard's own example.

Stewart Conn's 'The Barber-Surgeons to King James IV' demonstrates the antiquity of football in Scottish society and culture. The world's oldest football, made of leather with an inflatable pig's bladder inside, was found – where else? – but Stirling Castle, in the roof-space above the royal apartments. Since the roof-space was slated around 1540 the ball must have been lodged up there since before that time. It is furthermore recorded in the Court accounts of James IV for 11 April, 1497, that a sum was 'giffin to Jame Dog to by fut ballis to the King'. We can safely assume then that football was not the invention of *Sky Sports Live*, a fact further emphasised by two poems written in the 18th century by the Reverend John Skinner and Robert Fergusson.

Both of these poets use the popular 'voice' that was the hallmark of 'plebian play', or 'plebs at play' perhaps, known in the Scots literary tradition as 'Christis Kirk'. This is poetry written in common, vigorous Scots, the language that everyone in the 15th and 16th centuries spoke and wrote, if indeed they could write at all, including certainly the King and the Court Poets, or Makars, most notably Robert Henryson, William Dunbar and Sir David Lindsay. The vulgar tongue is therefore found alive and 'kicking', like everything else it seems, in 'The Christmass Bawing of Monimusk', 1739, written by the Reverend Skinner when he was 18 years old and an assistant schoolmaster in the said parish.

The football match described was not at all 'reverend', but a day-long joust between the local ploughmen and the townsfolk, played with all the grace and restraint of a Scottish Junior Cup-Final.

Skinner was a forerunner of Robert Fergusson who in 1765, wrote 'Elegy, On The Death Of Mr David Gregory, Late Professor of Mathematics in the University of St Andrews' when he was 14 years old and a student at St Andrews. The present Professor of Scottish Literature at St Andrews, the prominent scholar and poet Robert Crawford, considers that the sport alluded to in this poem is not football, but another ball-game that was peculiar to the University. This is a claim which your editor has unashamedly put aside for the far higher objective of claiming Robert Fergusson, who died in Bedlam in Edinburgh at the age of 24, for the Hall of Fame of Scottish Football and not just of Scots Poetry.

The 'game' of course includes 'sectarianism', hence the terracing 'anthems', 'The Fields of Athenry', adopted in the 1970s by the fans of Celtic FC and Liverpool FC, and 'The Sash', adapted about a century ago from the ballad 'Irish Molly-O', and sung regularly by followers of Rangers FC, though not exclusively. Snatches from the choruses of these songs might be familiar to the average reader of Scots poetry, but possibly not all of the words. Let these speak for themselves, as Dennis O'Donnell's wonderful 'Fid. Def.' does, whose protagonist is unwittingly caught up in Scotland's balefully ignorant sectarian communities. O'Donnell's poem speaks for most of 'us', the non-combatants, the non-sectarian, un-bigoted and largely non-religious majority who comprise modern Scotland.

There is of course another and much more benign populist tradition which has emerged in Scotland in recent years in direct opposition to the primitivism just touched on, namely, the open-handed zeitgeist of the Tartan Army – whose 'we are all Jock Tamson's bairns' philosophy shines through the essentially internationalist lyrics of Alasdair MacIver's 'Tartan Barmy'. From the ashes of the unrealistic hopes of World Cup success in Argentina in 1978, whipped up in part by the Scotland manager, Ally MacLeod, has emerged the phenomenon called 'The Tartan Army'. The football supporters of Scotland's national team, for whatever reason, and there may be many, have for the past three decades swapped the urge to conquer other nations on the field of play for the far less belligerent, much more sophisticated, and certainly much more life-enhancing goal of being invited along to 'the party' afterwards – anybody's 'party' – so long as it is not in Scotland – and so long as you can bring your own booze, your own kilt and your own conga.

All of the poems included have been written by Scots with a few exceptions: the Irish writer of 'The Fields of Athenry', Pete St. John, and the Irish-born but Edinburgh based Mike Dillon, author of 'Mick Turition'; the Australian poet, Rob Paraman, who wrote 'football god' while living in Glasgow; the Liverpudlian female poet, Parry Maguire, writes fittingly of Denis Law, Billy Bremner and Alex Young (the great Hearts and Everton mid-fielder) – who played the bulk of their illustrious careers in England, as indeed did Bill Shankly, whom Maguire also writes about – briefly and to the point, like the great man himself. Derek Bowman, author of 'Dad Before the Match', was born and brought up in Liverpool but spent his adult life in Scotland and wrote primarily for Scots literary magazines. The Left-wing poet (meaning politically Left), Adrian Mitchell, whose father was Scottish, is another kind of Anglo-Scot. An avowed Scotland supporter, Adrian contributes 'Golo, the Gloomy Goalkeeper'. No one could or should mistake Mike Harding for anything but a true-born Englishman, but the universality of his theme and the Scottish references in 'Daddy Edgar's pools' obviously warrants its inclusion, and the same goes for Sean O'Brien's 'Football! Football! Football!' Former poet-in-residence of Barnsley FC, Ian McMillan, who has an accent thicker than a Yorkshire spin-bowler, offers 'Somewhere on the South China Sea in 1938', a homage to his Carnwath-born, Third Lanark supporting father.

The already mentioned 'In the Bill Nicholson Suite' by Sarah Wardle serves to commemorate the late John White. Julia Darling was a poet and playwright who based herself in Newcastle so her 'World Cup Summer' refers to 'Big Jack' (Charlton), the Republic of Ireland manager in the 1990s. Big Jack was infamous for hard tackling and extending the eligibility criteria to allow any one who had ever bought a Val Doonican record to play for Ireland. The Scots too are a mongrel race, so Julia Darling's claim to be included in this anthology, based on a few lines from her poem 'Ancestry', seemed to this editor impossible to disregard:

My breasts are Scottish, from a line of sepia aunts,
who wrapped their Bristols tightly in sealing clothes,
with nipples as distant as Iona.

There is another 'minority' represented in this volume, poems by professional footballers, well, one, Billy Hunter, a Motherwell FC stalwart in the 1960s, who confirms that it really was 'a man's game' in 'Long Ago the Goalie's Fear'. I would describe myself as having loitered only briefly in the dressing-room of the senior professional game. At the tender age of 16 years, I became Bob Shankly's first signing for Hibernian FC when he took over as manager from Jock Stein in 1965. Always a part-timer, I was 'freed' three years later, never having made it out of the ranks of the hammer-throwers of the Scottish Junior League – which is the setting for 'Bag-men', a peon to the back-room boys of lower league football, whose many jobs include running onto the park during games to administer 'treatment', for want of a better term. Football was and is an occupation, an industry, with a largely hidden hinterland, whose origins were popular, local and communal rather than corporate and cosmopolitan, more Third Lanark than Champions League you might say, and this anthology wishes to remember that.

The Scottish Professional Footballers Association never really had to produce its own Milton. The 'beautiful game' or the 'poor man's ballet', as my father called it, recruited its own audience from the moment when school-boy legs, and some lassie legs too, a few, managed to whump the ball aloft, watched it soar through the air, land with a soft thud and then trickle satisfyingly towards the goal-line, usually marked by two jerseys thrown down in waste ground. For my generation, that was when the Faustian bargain with football was usually struck, the one which said that if you could turn into Denis Law, Jim Baxter or Jimmy Johnstone just long enough to produce that goal or deliver that ball into the penalty box at Hampden, then you would happily climb onto that rock beside Prometheus and have your livers chewed out every day for the rest of eternity by Arthur Montford[2].

[2] Arthur Montford: legendary 1960s–70s STV sports commentator, famous for wearing terrible large-check jackets and shouting incoherently whenever Scotland scored.

Football has always held a public space in Scotland, the kind usually reserved for politics, religion and warfare. The roar, and sway, of 'the crowd' has never been very far from the clichés of the fans, the players or the managers. The great Scot-Liverpudlian, Bill Shankly, the nearest the game has ever come to producing a philosopher, regarded football as a form of socialism, a team-game, in which everyone has a role and a part to play. Times change. Academic analysis would no doubt show that the game's metaphors changed as those generations, born around the Great War, began to die off. The exact date of their passing was probably 1978–9, the year the Devolution Referendum failed, Scotland exited early from the World Cup in Argentina, and Mrs Thatcher began limbering up on the track, preparing for yet another Tory come-back.

Yet some things abide. 1978 was also the year my father died, a personal and a symbolic demise, to me, of the fading away of the terracing generations, the flat-caps who survived two World Wars and National Health specs only to find themselves bundled out of the park by Mrs Thatcher, elbows flying. She would no doubt have elicited from them the same rueful cry that almost became the title of this anthology – 'never mind the ball (just get on with the game)' – a cry which one feels will last for as long as there is anyone left to play 'against', for as long as there is 'class', and for as long as there is 'society'. Or indeed, for as long as there is Poetry.

Alistair Findlay
October 2007
Bathgate

NOTE: the poems have been numbered 1–100 for ease of reference and in an order of reading proposed by the editor.

1

SCOTCH SOCCER
Alexander Scott

Robbery
wi' violence

2

THE BEWTEIS OF THE FUTE-BALL

Anonymous c. 1580

Brissit brawnis and broken banis,
Stryf, discord, and wastit wanis,
Crinket in eild, syne halt withall –
This are the bewteis of the fute-ball.

Twisted muscles and broken bones,
Strife, discord, and broken homes,
Old players stoop, their bodies stall –
These are the beauties of football.

3

GLASGOW, 1960
Hugh MacDiarmid

Returning to Glasgow after long exile
Nothing seemed to me to have changed its style.
Buses and trams all labelled 'To Ibrox'
Swing past packed tight as they'd hold with folks.
Football match, I concluded, but just to make sure
I asked; and the man looked at me fell dour,
Then said, 'Where in God's name are *you* frae, sir?
It'll be a record gate, but the cause o' the stir
Is a debate on 'la loi de l'effort converti'
Between Professor MacFadyen and a Spainish pairty.'
I gasped. The newsboys coming running along,
'Special! Turkish Poet's Abstruse New Song.
Scottish Authors' Opinions' – and, holy snakes,
I saw the edition sell like hot cakes!

4

DAD BEFORE THE MATCH

Derek Bowman

Taking the brute, he crouches down
And pumps and pumps the eager air
Into the dusty orange bladder
– Listen to it thrusting in! When
It's fit to burst, he bends the nipple
Over, ties it tight and tucks it in,
Threads the yellow lace and pulls
It to, knots it, stretches to his full
Height and flings the gleaming football – whang!
Down onto the flags. How clean it rang!
Bouncing my boyhood Saturdays miles high,
Way up into the clear blue sporting sky

5

UNRELATED INCIDENTS (4)
Tom Leonard

sittn guzz-
lin a can
a newcastle
brown wotchn
scotsport hum-
min thi furst
movement a
nielsens thurd
symphony – happy
iz larry yi
might say;

a wuz jist turn-
in ovir thi
possibility uv
oapnin anuthir
can whin thi
centre forward
picked up
a loose baw:
hi huddiz back
tay thi
right back iz
hi caught
it wayiz in-
step n jist
faintn this way

then this
way, hi turnd
n cracked it;
jist turnd n
cracked it;
aw nwan move-
ment; in ti
thi net.

6

From my Olympian view
Of the sabbuteo pitch

(Tonight, left to play on
Past bedtime)

I plotted the brilliant
Jinking run and chip

That would clinch it for Scotland
In the dying seconds.

Dad roared
And leapt over me

Towards the TV,
Out of his mind:

'YEAAHS! YA BEAUTY!'
(Chalmers had scored.)

Whimpering, I ran
For cover

To my mother's plaid hemline,
Having yet to learn

The depth and violence
Of the beautiful game.

BALL

Brian McCabe

The brown leather teamball
with the bootlaced mouth –
when it burst open in mid-air
the bladder's teat sprang out
and we headered a rubber udder.
It was as if all our mothers
had invaded the football pitch:
the porridge our studs made
in the goalmouth's mud
was part of a knitted balaclava
that surrounded every orifice.
That soup heavy with barley
left in the bottom of the bowl
made our hunger quicken
for the smell of slide-tackled earth,
pungent with victory or defeat.
When it was almost too dark
to see the ball, our names
came to claim us across the park
like those ghostly, neglected kids
who always turned up at the end
– wanting to know the score,
asking if there were any games.

8

EDWIN MUIR'S FURST FITBA

Liz Niven

Sae roon, sae saft
thi Orkney sun
on the green grun,
gliff o sunlicht
on steading door.

Bairn o seven dischairged
fae watching the slauchter.
Men yeuk like warriors,
a swine squeals atour the yerd
trotters clicking on corbled tiles.
Dirt fear flashin in its een,
a saw-like squaiking
fae the screed in its thrapple.

The skillet skailed, bluid struled
Sutherland cursed tae hae
sic reid hauns.
Hingin thro the sinnons
o its hin haughs,
harrigals fleitin in watter, entrails floating
the swine swayed
and the bern bauks creaked.

yeuk: yell; *atour*: across; *screed*: rip; *thrapple*: throat; *skillet*: pan; *skailed*: tipped; *struled*: streamed; *sinnons*: sinews; *haughs*: hams; *harrigals*: entrails; *fleitin*: floating; *bern beuks*: barn beams

Efter, bledder taen oot an
raised tae mooth,
it swelt gin till
they tethered it wae its thairm
an let it dry fur days.
Syne, kicked across the yerd
tae the boy, seik, scunnert,

'Here's yer baa, Edwin.'
Jist as yin day he'd be laith fu
at Glesca's mauk baneyerd
or Warsaw's weir teirin vennels.

A Fa indeed
sae sherp, sae herd.

---

bledder: bladder; *thairm*: guts; *syne*: then; *laith fu*: grueing; *mauk*: mucky;
weir teirin: war-torn; *Fa*: Fall, lost innocence

9

FIRST GEMME
Derek Ross

Stair Park, a cal December eftirnin,
Stranraer, at hame tae the micht o Forfar.
A'm nae mair than echt years al, an clingin
tae ma Granfether's han, stampin the glar
o mud an ash in an effort tae keep
warm. 'They're a team o triers, son, a team
o triers. Ye can ask nae mair', his heed
floatin on a sea o pipe smoke, his een
gleamin as he took the gemme in. Stranraer
won, twa nil. 'First gemme, eh, ye're ma lucky
mascot.' He bent doon, wrapped me in his scarf.
'A wee vict'ry son, jist a wee vict'ry.'
He spoke slow, so that A could unnerstan.
Granda, A miss yer voice, A miss yer han.

10

JAMES: FITBA DAFT

Janet Paisley

Some gemme, eh. Some gemme. Och, ah wis great.
Nippin aboot shoutin 'Ower here, ower here.
Pass ya wally.' Mind ah wis in some state.
Couldnae see me fur stoor – weel, akchully muck
cause it slaiggered the park an the waw roon aboot.
Bit it taks mair'n durt tae see me stuck.
You ask oor teechur, bit ah cannae hauf run.
Then wan eejit kicks the ba, a pass tae me.
Fair spiled ma fun. Bit there wis the goal
an there's naebody fur miles, right?
So ah goes like the clappers, it the speed o light.
The ref's runnin ahint. He's cheerin me oan.
Blawin his whistle, an ah'm keepin gaun.
Weel, it isnae ma faut ah kin stoap oan a peen.
Bit ah stoaps, jist like that, tae set up the baw
an the ref swerves tae avoid me, an runs intae the waw.
Wee Shug's in the goal an his mooth's hingin doon
cause he's watchin the ref crashin intae the brick.
Ah lit's fly. The ba's in!
Ah'll tell ye that wis some kick.
Ah'm punchin the sky, an jumpin aboot.
'Gemme's a bogey. See ra boy. That's ma goal. Yes!'
Then ower comes the ref, och he wis some mess.
There wis moss oan his eebroos, an bluid oan his shurt.
He looked awfy angry. Ah think that wis the durt.
Bit he taen a deep braith an lit go ae ma strip.
'Affside' he says. Ah says 'Aye ye wur, jist a bit'.

11

HERTS

James T. R. Ritchie

Herts are ages wi' the Castle Rock when there was nae
Castle even and the bees bummel'd owre fragrances
o' thyme and Troy stood still.

Herts bring back the vanished waters o' the Nor' Loch,
the waves wolterin' under the red October sun.

Herts dancin' oot is like merry flittin' o' folk long
ago through the bonny Netherbow Port that they ca'd
doun.

Herts mind us soberly of Flodden or Loos, or Dunbar
or the Dardanelles, a' that was leal and kind, lost and
forever.

But Herts is still Herts.

12

TWISTED KNEE
George Gunn

It began like this, I ran into John Knox, a fierce centre-half
I was coming out for this daft cross
(I was like that, a great young goalie)
it was mine all the way, but no, thump crash

The bastard twisted my knee right round
& I lay there screaming, eating grass
The trainer ran out & gave me the 'sponge'
John Knox said he was sorry really, was

going to pass back, we were on the same side
Centuries later, wiser now but alas
shouted at for staying on my line
I did my Italian goalkeeping, an elastic mass

of arms & legs leaping, punching, deflecting
'He's a guid keeper, bit frichtened o' the cross'
they said. Undeterred I soldiered on
with clean sheets & magic reflexes, the boss

between the posts, John Knox unfortunately became
team manager (now we never even won the toss)
we were stripped out in black, lost heart, skill
We all developed twisted knees, & alas

were relegated to the second
division, for ever, amen

13

THE BEST GOAL I HAVE EVER SCORED
Angus Peter Campbell

was at Peffermill in 1973
when I was George Best
and the ball was Mairi Mhòr
tied to the glorious curve of my ankle
I ran, for what must have been at least 50 years,
eclipsing past the cruel Duke and the cartons of Imperial Tea
my mother's note asking that they would oblige,
and there's a loaf, past it I go too
and suddenly there was a great space
as if Neil Armstrong had landed on the moon
only to find Denis Law there already
heading the sun into the far corner of the galaxy
and the ball unhindered and soaring,
the defenders cast meteorites,
15 years the ball soaring
eternally, no late tackle now possible,
the stilled moment soaring into sobriety with the defenders still
still,
the surrounding space enormous, beyond impair
that moment, the ball soaring
(from where white line meets white line)
to the precise top right hand corner
(where Puskas used to be)
and you there, on the edge of the field,
your Celtic scarf raised in glory
the alteration, the consummation, of the story.

14

THE DIFFICULTIES OF DISCIPLINE ON THE FOOTBALL FIELD

Brian Whittingham

The Teams
limber up for
their daily game
eating cheese pieces
and slugging
cans of tea.

The Park
stone cobbled pitch,
criss-crossed
railway lines,
a skin of icy snow.

The Kit
boots; steel toe capped,
strip; boiler suits in various
        stages of decomposition,
tracksuit; donkey jackets; overcoats
        that have known
        grander occasions,
ball; plastic (life span – extremely short).

The Play
Due to conditions underfoot
the teams move
in unison
as if the players' feet are
inter connected by a
linking mechanism,
like a toy football game
that will never catch on.

The Bevvie Merchants
are under
the illusion
that they are keeping
fit.

The Over-age Players
think
they can still
show the young team
a trick or two.

The Young Team
twist and turn
and dummy and swerve
and trap and
perform manoeuvres
which in their minds
are majestic
and in reality are sometimes
o.k.
and always likely to upset
the opposition,
especially.

The Conflict
of *Mad Shuggie McRitchie*
who knows that his defence
must stand steady
at all costs
as he stops Rab the Caulker
with a chest high
steel-toe-cap
that Rab takes exception to
and we know
because Rab proceeds to bounce
a loose cobble-stone
off Shuggie's forehead

and the crimson
stains the white

as the left winger
slots home the winner
and continues to run
towards the shed

The Final
Whistle
The 12:37 horn
signals the resumption
of building
ships.

15

ST MIRREN 3 ABERDEEN 1

Angus Peter Campbell

The date: 25 April 1959.
(I've checked!)

We stand outside
Taigh Dhòmhnaill Chorodail
(I remember),
as Bryceland, Miller, Baker and Baird scored.
(I phoned the sfa this morning and they told me.)

The wireless was in the window,
and at half-time we replayed the game
on the nearest patch of green, rocky grass.
(I recently saw how small, how very small, the patch was.)

The sun was shining, as it is today.

And the name Ian Ure,
that I've carried in my head
every moment of all my great pain
all these great, ridiculous, years.

16

from THE CHRISTMASS BAWING OF MONIMUSK, 1739

Reverend John Skinner

1

Has never in a' this country been
 Sic shoudering and sic fawing,
As happent twa, three days senseen,
 Here at the Christmass Ba'ing:
At evening syne the fallows keen,
 Drank till the neist day's dawing
Sae snell that some tint baith their een,
 And couldna pay their lawing
   For a' that day.

2

Like bumbees bizzing frae a bike,
 Whan hirds their riggin tirr,
The swankies lap thro' mire and slike,
 Wow! as their heads did birr:
They yowph'd the ba' frae dike to dike,
 Wi' unco speed and virr,
Some baith their shouders up did fyke
 For blythness some did firr
   Their teeth that day.

sic: such; *fawing*: falling; *senseen*: since; *syne*: then; *fallows*: fellows; *neist*:
next; *dawing*: dawning; *snell*: keen; *tint baith*: lost both; *lawing*: dues; *bike*:
hive; *hirds*: herders; *riggin tirr*: roofs strip; *swankies*: show-offs; *lap*: leap;
slike: mud; *birr*: birl; *unco*: amazing; *virr*: vigour; *fyke*: hitch; *firr*: grind

3

Rob Roy, I wot, he was na dull,
    His first loot at the ba',
And wi' a rap clash'd Geordy's skull,
    Hard to the steeple wa':
Wha was aside but auld Tam Tull,
    His frien's mishap he saw,
Syne brein'd like ony baited bull,
    And wi' a thud dang twa
        To th'yird that day.

29

The parish-clerk came up the yard,
    A man fou' meek o' mind,
Right jinsh he was and fell well fawr'd
    His claithing was fou' fine:
Just whare their feet the dubs had glaar'd
    And brew'd them a' like brine,
Daft Davy Don wi' a derf dawrd,
    Beft o'er the grave divine
        On's bum that day.

loot: boot; *brein'd*: bellowed; *yird*: earth; *jinsh*: spruce; *well fawr'd*: braw; *dubs*: mud; *glaar'd*: dirtied; *brew'd*: stained; *derf dawrd*: fierce dash; *beft*: knocked

In Monimuss was never seen
  Sae mony well beft skins,
Of a' the ba'-men there was nane
  But had twa bleedy shins:
Wi' streinzeit shoulders mony ane
  Dree'd penance for their sins,
And what was warst, scowp'd hame,
them lane,
    Maybe to hungry inns
        And cauld that day.

streinzeit: strained; *dree'd*: suffered; *scowp'd hame*: **scurried home**; *lane*:
alone; *inns*: dwellings

from BOYS: IN A CROWD

George Bruce

Run –
In some corner boys, men will be
Picking up their heels; in almost any
Small town on the map of our island
On a bright cold summer Saturday,
In a sea-town going to the local football match
With a crowd of blue-trousered men, all
Stockily built and lean, some bearded,
Some blue chinned, going to the big game.
They walk on the crown of the tarred streets,
Hands dropping easily at sides, or in pockets
To clicking turnstiles, or in, if they're players,
At the big gate. And not a handsbreadth off
Sunday psalms; and always about their ears
Boats bobbing, cascades of herring.

18

THE COMING OF THE WEE MALKIES
Stephen Mulrine

Whit'll ye dae when the wee Malkies come,
if they dreep doon affy the wash-hoose dyke
an' pit the hems oan the sterrheid light,
an' play wee headies oan the clean close-wa',
an' blooter yir windae in wi' the ba',
missis, whit'll ye dae?

Whit'll ye dae when the wee Malkies come,
if they chap yir door an' choke the drain,
an' caw the feet frae yir sapsy wean,
an' tummle thur wulkies through yir sheets,
an' tim thur ashes oot in the street,
missis, whit'll ye dae?

Whit'll ye dae when the wee Malkies come,
if they chuck thur screwtaps doon the pan,
an' stick the heid oan the sanit'ry man;
when ye hear thum come shauchlin' doon yir loaby,
chantin', *Wee Malkies*! *The gemme's ... a bogey*!
haw, missis, whit'll ye dae?

wulkies: cart-wheels

19

'THERE WAS THAT TIME CHARLIE TULLY'
Tom McGrath

there was that time charlie tully
took a corner kick
an' you know how he
wus always great at gettin thaem
tae curve in, well charlie takes the corner
and it curved in and fuck me did the wind
no cerry it right intae the net. but they
disputed it. and the linesman hud the
flag up and they goat away wae it and tully
hud tae take it again. an' fuck me does he no get
it in the net again. you should've
seen it. it just seemed tae go roon
in a kind o' hauf curcle. above aw their
heids. fuckin' keeper didnae know where tae look.
and there was that time john cassidy went into
the toilet and there was no
lightbulb and he just had to fix up with some
water he found in a bucket. and here it was piss.
he didnae discover it until it was actually in
him. he was very sick after that. he goat
very bad jaundice.

20

from KYND KITTOCK'S LAND
Sydney Goodsir Smith

This rortie wretched city
Built on history
Built on history
Born of feud and enmity
Suckled on bluid and treachery
Its lullabies the clash of steel
And shouted slogan, sits here in her lichtit cage,
A beast wi the soul o' an auld runkled whure,
Telling her billies o' her granderie in auld lang syne
– Oh ay, it was grand and glorious,
Splendant wi banners and nobilitie
– Nae greater granderie were was
Than was kent by thae grey stanes
But nou – juist memories for towrists – Ha!

rortie: huge and lying; *lichtit*: lighted

... Mock not, ye blythsome bairnies,
Mock not the men that biggit the land
Ye live by. Mock never the hands
That made these walls; mock never
The hands defended them. Mock not
That ye be not mocked in your turn
When your turn comes.
These men made siccar that ye walk the street the day –
Sae mock them nocht.
For you are history tae; yon's the rub.
See that ye mak mair siccar than your faithers did –
For time is short the day
And's gettin shorter as the hours flee.

Ane o' thae faces is a spaceman – or a millionaire maybe.
Ane is a captain o' men – or a bobby.
Ane will play for Hearts or Hibs, syne keep a pub,
And she the beauty-queen o' Portibellie without doubt –
– And mither o' five –

[verses, 2, 8, 9]

biggit: built; *siccar*: sure

21

from THE NEW DIVAN (86)
Edwin Morgan

Not in King's Regulations, to be in love.
Cosgrove I gave the flower to, joking, jumping down
the rocky terraces above Sidon, my heart bursting
as a village twilight spread its tent over us
and promontories swam far below
through goat-bells into an unearthly red.
He dribbled a ball through shrieking children and
they laughed at our bad Arabic, and the flower. To tell
the truth he knew no more of what I felt than of tomorrow.
Gallus, he cared little of that. I've not lost
his photograph. Yesterday, tomorrow
he slumbers in a word.

22

FITBAAER
Duncan Glen

I tell ye Jimmie
he's the greatest
              – – a naitural.

See him on the baa
the authority the arrogance
aabody can see it. The crood love
him. The world's aa his
and he taks it as his richt.

He gies them what they want.

And then the shirt aff
intae the bath – – and Jimmie
              wi his claes on

              that's him owre there
              sittin by himsel

You canna see it
but I tell ye Jimmie
       he's the greatest
              – – and that's him!

THE SPORTSMEN

Douglas Dunn

Scum, they have fast cars and money
And take other men's wives to play tennis.

They are always with us, making us laugh
At parties, in the pub. They live for prowess,

To be good at pastimes. Their times will come.
An ordinary man will beat them at their favourite games,

They will be murdered in bedrooms,
Their cars pressed into squares of scrap.

24

from OBAN 1955–1982
Iain Crichton Smith

'Sir, we are the stupid ones,' they say.
The football on the field invents a plot,
random and unpredicted. Who has taught
the inner rhythms of this outward play?

The English master with the grey moustache
watches from the touchline. 'Fodder, these …
But after all they rescued Rome and Greece
for the lucid talkers who turned pale as ash.'

Bewildering gyrations! On the wing
they flash fresh plumage, and the goal appears.
A ghost with gloves protects their universe.
The net behind him is a complex thing.

O graduate from this to Tennyson!
You fail at fences which the others raise.
We are practitioners of choice ideas.
It is our turn to listen and to learn!

TWO SKILLS

William Neill

Alas! said Balefire, if instead of Greek
asclepiads and Latin prosody,
better by far had I been left to be
a budding forward in our shabby street,
a tattered tennis ball beneath my feet.
But I was told to win a scholarship
drag myself by my bootstraps to the tip
of middle-class esteem, a joy complete.

Hero of millions now, my childhood friend,
earns in a day more than my annual fee.
Supporters worship dressed in scarf and bonnet.

A skill in footwork was his only end.
Look what the grammar school has done for me:
a fiver cheque for lining out a sonnet.

26

ALEX YOUNG

Parry Maguire

'The Golden Vision'
Spreading passes
With eyes closed
The partnership with Vernon
Blessed with titles
Blessed with glory
And the silent earth
Refused to give up
Your footprints
So that no one else
Could trace the genius
Of your steps

BILLY BREMNER

Parry Maguire

The man with the double-barrelled heart
Whose single-minded soul
Knew no other road
No song to sing
Boots bereft of hesitation
Deficit of fear
And long, long on cause

28

from ELEGY, ON THE DEATH OF MR DAVID GREGORY, LATE PROFESSOR OF MATHEMATICS IN THE UNIVERSITY OF ST ANDREWS

Robert Fergusson

Now mourn, ye college masters a'!
And frae your een a tear lat fa,
Fam'd Gregory death has taen awa
   Without remeid;
The skaith ye've met wi's nae that sma,
   Sin Gregory's deid.

Weel vers'd was he in architecture,
An' kent the nature o' the sector,
Upon baith globes he weel could lecture,
   An gar's tak heed;
Of geometry he was the Hector;
   But now he's deid.

Sae weel's he'd fley the students a',
Whan they war skelpin at the ba,
They took leg bail and ran awa,
   Wi pith and speed;
We winna get a sport sae braw
   Sin Gregory's deid.

skaith: loss; *baith globes*: sky and earth; *leg bail*: flight

Great 'casion hae we a' tae weep,
An' cleed our skins in mourning deep,
For Gregory death will fairly keep
    To take his nap;
He'll till the resurrection sleep
    As sound's a tap.
                    [verses 1, 5–7]

JIMMY JOHNSTONE
(*from Football Triptych*)
Alan Bold

See him swerving on the ball
Perfect balance, armed with all
Athletic graces. Now he shoots,
The ball spins from his magic boots.

He has been compared to men
Twice his age, then half again.
Morton, Matthews, Georgie Best,
Dixie Dean – you know the rest.

But who has quite his dribbling powers,
His ability to run for hours?
Who can match, for sheer control,
His motives as he moves for goal?

COMPOSERS OF MUSIC
Norman MacCaig

Musicians, calling in your circles and phases,
helpless in their ruminant fire,
unable to speak anything
but the laws of miracles,
how can you fail to shed
your tremulous humanity? How can you carry
your spongebag heart, your tick-tocking brain
along those orbits where you go
without skidding – without dying
into the clusters of notes you explode
in the earth's dark mind?

– I regard you with joy and with envy
from my thicket of words.

31

PARISH FOOTBALL
Christopher Salvesen

Out then we strode on the tussocky field-slope ready for
    battle,
Foresters versus the Farmers, a game to involve all the
    valley.
Hard it was fought in the echoing sunlit quiet of the
    evening,
Shoulders and foreheads opposed in hard knocks, not a
    shin without bruises,
Held in a pattern of dark green trees
(Dragooned right enough, a bit on parade)
And the luminous swelling khaki-coloured hills
(Where once the Legions stumbled –
Though only on punitive raids or particularly imprudent
    patrols).
I played on the side of the forest
(Was that the right side to be on –
The Sitka spruce instead of the Blackface?)
Wore just my shoes, tied on with binder twine,
Went over once on my ankle,
Made, a heroic moment, a goal-line clearance.
We won 2–0.

Another time I was goalie –
Custodian: a word barely existing
Outside the columns of 'Ossian'
And his colleagues.
But – a man who defends, a keeper
Of place: that pine-clad valley
As it cradled the evening air,
Cool, lambent (that's really the word),
Of resin and slanting sunlight.

Jimmy Cowan, Morton and Scotland goalkeeper,
Died aged 41
A *Times* obituary too
Albeit brief
(None of your 'Ossians' there):
Just after the war, at Somerset Park,
Ayr United at home to Morton
We stared close-up from behind the goal – the home
   'keeper was
Skinny, starved, with a little moustache,
And a raw red nose (with a drip on) –
Pinched and unwell in a hairy grey jersey.
He let five in:
'Five shots they had – and five goals!'
But Cowan – 'safe as a bank',
How healthy he looked,
Well-fed, 'thighs like barrels',
His yellow jersey fitting like a pelt.
Masterful, he drew a mark with his heel
From the penalty-spot to the six-yard line
To get his positioning right –
Controversial it was, against the rules, but
The goalmouth was his,
He commanded his area …

LONG AGO THE GOALIE'S FEAR

Billy Hunter

Long ago the goalie's fear,
Wiz centre-forwards in the clear,
Roarin' thru, they'd shoot the ba',
Then keep on goin', the sight wiz braw.
Shoulder tae shoulder they baith wid meet,
The goalie wiz normally knocked off his feet,
Intae the net wi' the ba' in his hands,
'A goal', said the ref, 'Great', said the fans.
Now wi' the goal-tenders poncin' about,
No one can touch them, or they're up the spout,
They'll end up wi' lipstick and vanity bag,
The excitement has gone, now it's a drag.

Wings disappeared when they brought in the flanks,
Instead of wee wingers we now have the tanks,
Mid-fielders and full-backs, who get the ba' wide,
Cross tae the pie-man, who's not on their side,
The runnin', the jumpin', and tacklin' improves,
But where are the back-heels, the dummies, the moves,
The flicks and the one-twos, are things of the past.
Tae be at the top now, ye've got tae be fast.

ROBBIE
Donny O'Rourke

We shouldered you out into a cold blue morning,
the pig iron kind all keepers hate

when limbs get skinned and balls bounce high.
There was a cross wind blowing from the Forth –

a day for inswingers; though corners
never troubled you who'd have got both hands

on the moon, given a two yard run at it.
No, your weakness was the fierce first timer

cleverly kept down, the only way we ever
got you out, playing 'Three and In',

on your well kept Gourock lawn,
replaying the war years

when you were Cappielow's number one,
saving penalties like ration coupons.

To the Telegraph then, Robbie,
you were Morton's Miracle Man Between The Sticks,

invincible in polo neck and bunnet –
old goalie a league of ailments

couldn't beat, till a cunning cancer
aimed one low.

34

JIM LEIGHTON
Matthew Fitt

creesh on the ba
ren skelpin doon
the field aa slidderie
unner the lichts

he kens
athoot bein tellt, he kens

oot ther in the soss
oot ther in the stoor
the ba skyters yin wey
is blootert the ither
a man is cowped

in the thringin stand
the ghaists greet an rair
the trachle o buits
breenges on

an he kens
athoot bein tellt, he kens

the ba braks
fae the midden
is gaithert
lyk a perlie
chistit doon
is trappt
a wee flick on

his hert
stoonds
his jaa
gaes ticht
his rauchle haun
maks a nieve in its glove

whit wey it is sair
whit wey it is toom
whiy wey it is in the lane cauld nicht
he kens

syne a touch
a flick
the laddie's bate
the fuhl-back's skinned
the defence is left haunless
juist the keeper
ainlie the keeper

an the keeper stauns
at the creel o the goal
glaur on his pus
an his een bleezin
his mooth aa dreh
aff a drooth he canna
shak these days

hero or cuddie
the fishwifes blaw
yet the chanterin rair
o the cronies in the stand
sall no him unhool
sall naethin him daunt

straucht an smert
the ba is lowsed
sherp as a skelf
burlin aa weys
a buhlitt

swippert, eident
shair
yin gret lowp
the keeper hurls
his bow-hochd banes
intil ae lang unfankilt airch
raxin
till his jyntes crackil
an gits
haurdlie
no even a haill
fingir
tae it

skelp
aff the bar
the ba on the grund
buits flingin, breengin in
knee in the baas
a clout on the heid
syne the keeper hes it, hauds it
the ba in his airms
snod and sauf
lyk a puir unhovin bairn

whit wey it is sair
whit wey it is toom
whit wey it is the lane caald nicht
he kens

an the chanter o the ghosties
nor the fishwifes in the stand
or the sooch o the deevil hissel
sall no him unhool
sall naethin him daunt

the keeper
chaas his chewnie
draps the ba on the flair
an wi a glower o pure smeddum
blooters hit richt
back intil
the thrawn, raivelt, maikless gemm

35

JOHNNY THOMSON[1]
William Hershaw

Johnny Thomson, lithe as Spring
An athlete and a goalkeeper
Wha could save onythin'
But wan wanchancy kick tae the heid
And the lave o a young life
Gi'en scant time tae floor.

Yet ye can still fund auld men
Wha walked tae his funeral in Cardenden
Wha's faces wull bloom owre and een
Moisten at memries o days lichtened;
Brocht fae Brigton, means test and dole
Bi his gracefu dives and shut-oots.

Johnny Thomson, in the thirties
Mindid naethin' fir politics or bigotry
And lay deein at Ibrox park;
Ahent him at the Rangers' en'
The hoots and jeers grouwin like weeds
Wad hae drooned oot the crood at Nuremberg.

lave: rest

[1] Celtic goalkeeper in the 30s accidentally killed diving at the feet of
   Sam English, the Rangers centre-forward

36

from JANUARY THE TWENTY-FIFTH
George MacKay Brown

I

The old men said the name Robbie Burns
    As if he'd farmed
Very recently, in Cairston or Stenness or Hoy.

What a man, what a man! They said
    Shaking their heads, smiling.
    What a man for the drink!
What a man for the lassies!

It was of the utmost importance
    That Robbie was a poor man
Like themselves: a toil-bent farmer.

There might be a Barleycorn pause
    Between a quote and a stave of song.
The women, they never seemed
    To give a moment's thought to that poet.

II

The Hamnavoe kids groaned inwardly. There
    On their open books
Was a new poem nailed to the page
    To a Mouse:
'To be learned by heart,' said the teacher.

Words like thistles and thorns
They ploughed through the winter language
    And pity ran for cover
    This way and this, and entered
A few small cold wondering hearts.

III

They moved in the schoolroom
    Among heroic images,
The Bruce at Bannockburn under the shouting castles

Mary Queen of Scots
    Inside that English castle
    First in her black gown, then the red,
    Then block and axe and blood.

Bonny Prince Charlie at Holyrood, dancing –
    On the rainlashed moor
    Turning a horse's head into the west –
    An old broken king at the brandy bottle
    In a foreign castle.

Now this ploughman shaken with song and love
    Among stones and furrows.

IV

There was another hero, more marvellous even
    Than Bruce or Burns.

He too died in the glory of the field
    Young and beautiful
    John Thomson, goalkeeper of Celtic.
For the boys of Hamnavoe
Football was war, was magic, and chant.
A star glittered and went out.

37

GOLO, THE GLOOMY GOALKEEPER
Adrian Mitchell

Golo plays for the greatest soccer team in the Universe.

They are so mighty that their opponents never venture out of
their own penalty area.

They are so all-conquering that Golo never touches the ball during
a match, and very seldom sees it.

Every game seems to last a lifetime to Golo, the Gloomy Goalkeeper.

Golo scratches white paint off the goalposts' surface to reveal the
silver shining underneath.

He kisses the silver of the goalpost.

It does not respond.

Golo counts the small stones in the penalty area.

There are three hundred and seventy eight, which is not his lucky
number.

Golo pretends to have the hiccups, then says to himself, imitating
his sister's voice:

Don't breathe, and just die basically.

Golo breaks eight small sticks in half.
Then he has sixteen very small sticks.
He plants geranium seeds along the goal-line.
He paints a picture of a banana and sells it to the referee at half-time.

Golo finds, among the bootmarks in the dust, the print of one
    stiletto heel.
He crawls around on all fours doing lion imitations.
He tries to read his future in the palm of his hand, but forgets to
    take his glove off.
He writes a great poem about butterflies but tears it up because
    he can't think of a rhyme for Wednesday.
He knits a sweater for the camel in the Zoo.

Golo suddenly realises he can't remember if he is a man or a woman.
He takes a quick look, but still can't decide.
Golo makes up his mind that grass is his favourite colour.
He puts on boots, track-suit, gloves and hat all the same colour as
    grass.
He paints his face a gentle shade of green.

Golo lies down on the pitch and becomes invisible.
The grass tickles the back of his neck.
At last Golo is happy.
He has fallen in love with the grass.
And the grass has fallen in love with Golo, the Gloomy
    Goalkeeper.

38

JOCK STEIN
Raymond Vettese

Deed in harness, deed in harness,
'one match too many' the man said,
and mebbe sae – yet ilka match
gaithert Scotland as nocht else did,
as nocht else, it seems, can,
Nine meenits left – Dave Cooper's penalty
the score level an' thoosans o banners
an' skye-wurd voices roarin his name
and his hairt aboot tae explode.
Cairried awa helpless, the camera
catched his laist look back on the place
o triumph an' disaster, whar millions
had cheered, had grat –
Greet for Scotland that winna come again,
greet for things that winna return,
greet for the suddenness o daith,
but mind whan Celtic
won the European Cup
Bill Shankly cried oot; 'John, ye're immortal!'

39

COTHROM PEANAIS
MAR CHUIMHNEACHAN AIR JOCK STEIN
Cailein MacFhionghain

An oidhch'ud
an dèidh naidheachd do bhàis
sann shil deòir a' bhròin 'nan sruth
troimh làrach deòir an aoibhneis
air aodainn do luchd-leanmhainn
gun smaointinn no gun suathadh.

Ach bidh cuimhn' ort gu bràth, Jock,
oir thug thu misneachd do na mìltean
agus na seòid anns na cearclan uaine,
's chan fhacas an leithid bhon uair sin.

Bu tu 'n gaisgeach, Jock, a thairg gu h-iomlan
do chorp fhèin is d' inntinn
gus an dùthaich umhail seo a chur an àird;

's gu dearbh cha robh sinn airidh ort
a dh'eug gu glòrmhor, grad,
an dèidh faochadh fadalach
an idhch' ud.

PENALTY
IN MEMORIAM OF JOCK STEIN
(translation)
Colin MacKinnon

That night
after the news of your death
the tears of grief poured in streams
through the traces of the tears of joy
on the faces of your followers
unfeigned and unwiped.

But you will always be remembered, Jock,
for you inspired thousands
and the warriors in the green hoops,
and their like has not been seen since then.

You were the hero, Jock, who devoted completely
your own body and your mind
to lifting up this humble land;

and indeed we didn't deserve you
who died gloriously, suddenly,
after belated relief
that night.

PENALTY

G. F. Dutton

Natural
to play football
in a flat land

pointed and planned,
where streets invite
anguish at edges, wounds

from whatever surrounds.
Inevitable
some Saturday night

to come by a ball
that would bounce and roll
far on the flat

and to stop all that,
teach it drill,
trap it, keep it,

spot-lit, still,
sized for a goal.
And only fair

to play it square,
even the score.
To kick by rule

strike that ball, net it while
cries rain down and
streamers fall

acknowledging out of the darkness.
They cheer us yet, gather about our
stamping and mismanaged feet.

MEN MONOLOGUE: ANNEMARIE
Liz Lochhead

Men see men I've had it
Up to here absolutely
It's all off completely.
I said suppose that'll suit you fine I said
You can go out with your mates
Every night of the week and not just Thursdays
I said,
Look at the state of you
The beer's all going to your belly already
And coming from the West of Scotland you
Are statistically unlikely
Even to reach the age of 25
Without false teeth
And to tell the truth
Since we got engaged
You never bother with the Brut
Or the good suit I said
I'm sick to the backteeth of
Every time we go for a Chinese
You order
Chicken and chips, fried egg and peas.
I said No way
Believe me the only way I'd ever consider
The World Cup in Mala-bloody-ga
For my honeymoon
Is if I was guaranteed
An instant trade you in for a

Six foot shit-hot sharp shooter that never failed to hit
the spot.
I told him where to stick his bloody
One carrot diamond-is-forever.

I blame his mother.

42

DON'T CRY FOR ARGENTINA FOR ME
Alastair Mackie

It's nae o Argentina that I mind o
aifter aa the play was played. (Their forwards
wi their hell-black manes wallopin the air.)
Nor Brazil passin their triangles as trig
as Euclid's. Na, nor ony o the goals
ootside the box, wi men haudin themsels,
and the haill line strung oot like washin.
Na. It's o Airchie Gemmell's feet steekin
a pattren on the selvage o the box.
His skeely needle threidit the ba past
three men, their legs begowkit by the phantom darner.
It was a baldy-heidit goblin scored the goal.
His shot a rainbow, airches owre his name.

43

ARGENTINA 1978
Ron Butlin

A ship lies gasping in the cupboard:
its crew disturbs my sleep night after night
with their demands to put to sea.

– But no sooner do I close my eyes
and start imagining to myself the long ball
from Bruce Rioch that I take past one man, side-
flick past a second and am lining up for a Peter Lorimer-
rocket-postage-stamp in the top right-hand corner
while the crowd goes wild, wild, wild
– when from behind the terraces I hear the opening strains
of the first of that evening's many sea-shanties.

I try to ignore it, and tell myself that back home
all Scotland's sitting boozed and bonneted in front of the TV,
watching me with only the goalie to beat
and the World Cup as good as on the mantelpiece.

– But already the crowd's been infiltrated;
already some of them
(I suspect the ones with eye-patches,
and anchors over their shoulders)
have started singing 'Hearts of Oak'
in counterpoint to the crowd's roar
– and I see the goal-posts and netting sway gently
in an easterly breeze.

I try to ignore it for the ball's still at my feet
and I tell myself that back home
all Scotland's standing on the sofas and the sideboards
cheering themselves tartan.

– But already the Easterly has freshened up,
the goal-posts are listing slightly
and, as the netting billows, are pulling away from the terraces
where *everyone's* now wearing an eye-patch
and has an anchor over his shoulder
– some of them are even watching the game through telescopes!

I try to ignore them and line up the ball for the big one,
the one that's going to be the one and only,
the most beautiful thing to come out of Scotland
since McEwan's Export,
the one they'll action-replay till the film falls apart.

The crowd gives out with 'Steady boys, steady!'
I try to ignore it
– the ball turns into a pink bobbing marker-buoy!
I try to ignore it
– the goals are towing the terraces of shantying sailors
out to sea!
I try to ignore it:
Scotland's not going to be robbed, not this time!

Then suddenly I am alone in Argentina.
No crowd, no ball, no goals, no cup.
The grass is turning to sea-water
– and it's a long swim home!

44

ANDY GRAY
Alan Bold

As a matter of fact
Strikers are made for impact
And they don't make them
Any more powerful
Or lethal
Than Andy Gray.
His durability
Takes him through the match,
And we watch
As he lurks
In the goalmouth, works
His passage to the front
Then, in a blinding flash,
Crash!
He materialises from somewhere
And powers through the air
To send the keeper reeling
And the ball smack
In the back of the net.
He's bulky
Yet crafty
As a fox,
With a feeling
For the killer-goal.

Deadly in the box
Andy Gray
Stalks
His prey:
He's like
A predator poised to strike.

WHAT THE CROWD SAID

William McIlvanney

This is the sound of our lives, it said,
This outrage that falls like a thunderbolt
From the clouds of confusion we live in, this,
This is the baby we found dead,
The no-hope job and the flea-pit bed.
This is the mugging at night in the street
While the nice people pass in their cars, the sound
Of the violent quarrel we heard through the wall.
This is the ground shifting under our feet.
Strip off the social lies, this is all
We see all around. This is our fate.
This is the space in the questionnaire
We didn't fill in, exhalation of air
We have to breathe, the quick disco knives,
The children in care, the political smiles.
This is the dole where we lost our wives.
This is contempt for the government's wiles.
This is the word to describe our lives.

The referee, versed in tones of howl,
Made an instant free translation: foul.

46

ALBA V ARGENTINA, 2/6/79
(mios as deidh Taghadh na Parlamaid, 3/7/79)
Ruaraidh MacThòmais

Glaschu a' cur thairis
le gràdh dùthcha,
leòmhainn bheucach
air Stràid an Dòchais,
an Central
mùchte le breacan,
cop air Tartan bho mhoch gu dubh,
is mùn nam fineachan air a' bhlàr;
iolach-catha a' bàthadh bùrail nam busaichean –
Sco-o-t-land, Sco-o-t-land –
Alba chadalach,
mìos ro fhadalach.

SCOTLAND V ARGENTINA, 2/6/79
(*a month after the General Election, 3/5/79*)
(*translation*)
Derick Thomson

Glasgow erupting
with patriotism,
growling lions
on Hope Street,
the Central
choked with Tartan,
foaming from dawn to dusk,
and clansmen's piss on the battlefield;
the battle-cry drowning the buses' drone –
Sco-o-t-land, Sco-o-t-land –
sleepy Scotland,
a month late.

47

JOHN KENNEDY, STEELWARKER, 1939–1975
Duncan Glen

The haill warld kens o Celtic Park Football Ground.
Pass it by. Pass through the grey canyons that are homes.

Suddenly you are at the warks. Clyde Iron Works
jined to Clydebridge Steel Works across the river
and the Foondry doon the road at Tollcross.

Ahint the black pooer o the warks aw would seem desolation,
filth, and scrub and rubbish
– but here the tanner-baw helped build Celtic Park's fame.

A daurk Clyde meanders through
aboot to cam to a stop in some underworld, it seems.
Yet it has its pastures even in this depressed land.

A solitary carronade wi cannonbaw stuffed in its mooth
made to defend thae shores frae Napoleon
pints oot across the bosses' caur park.

Napoleon never cam, nor the Kaiser, nor Hitler.
Aw warked for you could say.

Noo aw's for scrap.

'You canna expect a job for ever,' says John Kennedy.

48

THE GOOD THIEF

Tom Leonard

heh jimmy
yawright ih
stull wayiz urryi
ih

heh jimmy
ma right insane yirra pape
ma right insane yirwanny us jimmy
see it nyir eyes
wanny uz

heh

heh jimmy
lookslik wirgonny miss thi gemm
gonny miss thi GEMM jimmy
nearly three a cloke thinoo

dork init
good jobe theyve gote the lights

I THINK JESUS WOULD HAVE BEEN AT IBROX

(*Scottish minister*)

Alastair Mackie

'Jesus at Ibrox'? Christ!
I can jist see the saviour o the world
staunin in the terrace in his Jewish goun
raxin his hands ower that toozled sea
o Union Jacks and scarves and cairry-oots
and cryin 'Peace be still'
    Of coorse,
he'd be joukin the halo o screw-taps
    roond his heid.
Next on his knees, tastin his broken teeth,
while 'Peeth be thtill' kept bleedin fae his mooth.
And then the boots gaed in, his body kickit
like a tanner-ba in some close-neid game.
    O aye boys,
Jesus widda been at Ibrox, I'm telling ye.
He'd hung on Calvary aince, hadn't he?
    He kent the score.

CRACK

Tom Leonard

cuts inty thi box
croass cumzthi centre hoff
a right big animull

crack

doon goes Dalgleesh
ref waves play on
nay penahlti

so McNeill complainzty im
oot cumzthi book

tipicl
wan mair upfurthi luj

FID. DEF.

Dennis O'Donnell

Saturday evening, just out of Confession,
buoyed with the lightness of Sanctifying Grace,
walking up the street, who should I bump into
but 'Sojer' Bishop with his big, beery face,
his Rangers scarf brandished above his head,
a vivid sash of blue, white and red.

'Hello! Hello! We are the Billy boys!'
You could see in his eyes that, from 3 till half 4,
he had been up to the knees in Fenian blood;
there had been No Surrender, as in days of yore;
that old Derry walls had been stoutly guarded.
He was the one I feared most – the hardest

of all the knobbly Protestant boys.
'Haw-heh, shitehouse! Ur yew a Fenian?'
I had never heard the term in my life,
but, from the look on his face, I could easily have been one.
I guessed 'Fenian' meant the same as 'Pape',
which I certainly was. How to escape?

'Naw, Sojer,' says I, 'ahm a Protestant, me.
God bless King Billy and FTP'
'Gaun yersel, wee man.' He lurched away down the road,
and I stood there, having denied my God.
Oh, agony of remorse! And guilt even sharper,
not to have suffered the death of a martyr.

But that soon passed. This was Bathgate, not Rome.
So I treated myself to a white pudding supper
and scoffed it in the back of the bus going home.

52

THE FIELDS OF ATHENRY
Pete St. John

By a lonely prison wall, I heard a young girl calling
'Michael, they have taken you away
For you stole Trevelyan's corn
So the young might see the morn
Now a prison ship lies waiting in the bay.'

Low lie the fields of Athenry
Where once we watched the small free birds fly
Our love was on the wing
We had dreams and songs to sing
It's so lonely round the fields of Athenry.

By a lonely prison wall, I heard a young man calling
'Nothing matters, Mary, when you're free
Against the famine and the crown
I rebelled, they cut me down
Now you must raise our child with dignity.'

By a lonely harbour wall, she watched the last star falling
As the prison ship sailed out against the sky
For she'll live in hope and pray for her love in Botany Bay
It's so lonely round the fields of Athenry.

53

THE SASH MY FATHER WORE

Anonymous c. 1905

Sure I'm an Ulster Orangeman, from Erin's Isle I came,
To see my British brethren all of honour and of fame,
And to tell them of my forefathers who fought in days of yore,
That I might have the right to wear, the sash my father wore!

It was old but it was beautiful, and it's colours they are fine
It was worn at Derry, Aughrim, Eniskillen and the Boyne.
My father wore it as a youth in bygone days of yore
And on the twelfth I love to wear the sash my father wore.

For those brave men who crossed the Boyne have not fought or
 died in vain
Our Unity, Religion, Laws, and Freedom to maintain,
If the call should come we'll follow the drum, and cross that river
 once more
That tomorrow's Ulstermen may wear the sash my father wore!

And when some day, across the sea to Antrim's shore you come,
We'll welcome you in royal style, to the sound of flute and drum
And Ulster's hills shall echo still, from Rathlin to Dromore
As we sing again the loyal strain of the sash my father wore!

JOHN KNOX IS WATCHING THE CELTIC MATCH

Alistair Findlay

John Knox is watching
the Celtic Match: 'Come on Porto,' he prays, and
asks the Lord's forgiveness for cheering on the
    lesser of the two

sin-begotten sperms
of the Jezebel of Rome, Hell's cast-offs, hardly a
blade of grass between them, in the Debauchery
    stakes, gangrel seedlings

frae the fell gash
of Papistry that's met it's match, thank Christ, in
the portals of the SFA, the Rock, the Hard Place,
    the Eternal Standing

Stone of Protestant
Redemption, and may the Lord be Thankit to this
day for the likesy Willie Allison, the scourge o'
    Tattie-munchers

everywhere,
who are allowed the vote now, and to subscribe
to Sky-Sports-Live, but John is in a good mood,
    half-time,

Celtic down,
he allows himself a pie, and a chat with Donald
Findlay cheers him up, then Larsson strikes,
    then Porto's up,

    then Larsson strikes again,
then Bobo Baldy, an Instrument of Christ, tho'
French, gets ordered off and John's gone nuts
    for Porto's won the Cup,

    and order's been restored
to the Kingdom of the Lord: John offers up
a prayer for the return of Stein, the Renegade,
    who left the fold.

55

IDENTITY LEAGUE
Robert Crawford

Duns Scotus	1	Harristotelian Ravers	1
Echt Weecaledonians	1	Scots Internationalists	1
Cock o' the South	1	Orkney Vagina Academicals	1

In Kirrie, where they sell hand-painted lightbulbs,
In St Andrews, where St Andrew never preached,
Through vennels, kennels, bennels, shrines and hoolies,
From California Hall to Moscow, Ayrshire,
The needle match between Scotland and Scotland
Goes into extra time and never stops.

56

TARTAN BARMY
(tune: 'Bonnie Dundee')
Alasdair MacIver

There's some think we're crazy, there's some think we're daft,
But win, lose or draw we will have the last laugh,
We'll never forsake you, back you to the hilt,
With a skirl o' the pipes and a swing o' the kilt.

Come lift up your cup, come lift up your can,
Resplendent in tartan, every loyal fan,
We go all o'er Europe and drink the pubs dry,
Oh, there's nobody like us, we're Scots you and I.

So dust down your bonnet and buckle your belt,
Lace your brogues tightly and straighten your kilt,
There's beer to be drunk and there's songs to be sung,
Our fame it proceeds us, the night is yet young.

The thistle's our flower, the Saltire our flag,
Our lion is rampant – there's only one snag,
We're better at singing than kicking a ball,
We're everyone's friend but we'll ne'er win fuck all.

So wherever you wander be sure and stand tall,
Keep a smile and a handshake to greet one and all,
And whatever befalls us there's one thing that's sure,
We've gone Tartan Barmy and there is no cure.

MICK TURITION
Mike Dillon

Nine pints into the evening
beneath the nicotine ceiling
of a Drongan bar and there's
poems in every smoke ring
when suddenly
it's the bells
    the bells
    the last bell
and your tongue slips into the
brogue and it fits like a glove
and now a man cud doiya torsht
and nowan wud care and jazzes
Mary and Joseph but I'm desperate
for micturition

And there's sweet relief waiting
in the cludge and you're drowning
flies and making thunder all along
the stained steel urinal when you
    sense
    a presence
    and there it is

18 stone of pig-eyed
FTP fundamentalism
    wading over to you
    18 stone of redhand
and godsaprod tattoos
    bearing down on you
    18 stone of bluenose
rightfoot magahun

HEY, PAL! YOU IRISH?

You zip your fly
look it in the eye
say, NAW NO ME PAL
and you're away out whistling
Derry's wall and faraway
in some Calvinist farmyard
a cock crows once
twice
thrice

58

from SITUATIONS THEORETICAL AND CONTEMPORARY
Tom Leonard

You have returned to Glasgow after a long exile.
A *Glasgow Herald* special edition is selling like hot cakes.
It publishes a Turkish poet's abstruse new song.

This Turkish poet is of an international cast of mind.
He also has an unselfconscious enjoyment of working-class
    culture.
In fact his song is about a match between Glasgow Celtic and
    Glasgow Rangers.

A certain Professor MacFadyen has detected the influence of
    MacDiarmid.

59

THE BARBER-SURGEONS TO KING JAMES IV

Stewart Conn

We the Barber-Surgeons of Edinburgh, gratified at the granting
of the Council's Seal of Cause, applaud your Majestie's probings
into the workings of the body, its ailments and cures. Neither
blood-letting, nor amputation and excision, lightly undertaken.
Yet the climate one of suspicion, witness Robert Henryson's
'Sum Practysis of Medecyne', scurrilously deriding *lechecraft*
and *feisik* alike – and by insinuation ourselves. Were we to wield
our instruments as he does his quill, the cleansing Water of Leith
would soon be the River Lethe. That said, as much quackery
in his calling as among our fellows: how many makars
worth their salt – most seeking truth through verse as likely
to find it up their erse. Mercifully not all tarred, with the one
brush ... Were we the fraudulent cuckoo-spits he suggests,
we might belabour him with reciprocal curses. Suffice
to say his legal brethren in Dunfermline can keep him.
On another tack, Majestie, a modest plea. Pledged to honour
our calling in time of strife and plague, we are sore put upon
mending cracked skulls and broken shins from the fiery
pursuit of fute-ball. If not banned (or the worst hackers
booted out) could we humbly petition for a royal decree
preserving Holyrood Park for the more seemly sport of archery?

60

THE SCOTTISH JUNIOR CUP FINAL
John McCaughie

and it's doun tae
Cumnock Juniors and Auchinleck Talbot
in the final
and it's no jist anither gemme
for the supporters
it's High Noon
it's showdown at the OK Corral
and for the players
it's time for an early blood-bath

and we're standing on the terraces
singing
Away the 'Nock, Away
and shouting
and cursing
at everything and everytime
Talbot get the baw

and it's do or die
and Cumnock's yin doun
wi five minutes left on the clock
– no counting injury time –
so that's another twenty minutes, easy

and it's life or death
then the Talbot do the dirty again
and score
a shite goal that was a mile offside
the chant goes up
bastards bastards bastards
and the pies fly
and the fists and the feet and the teargas
and it's enough to make you greet

when oot the blue
it's in the net – the Talbot's
a divin heider
and there's time left yet
for a miracle
you can feel it in your bones
then this cross gets turned intae a goal
and it's kill or be killed
as another player is stretchered aff
then there's a player that's been asleep
for maist o the gemme
a flash o genius
and he's away up the wing
like a man possessed
his cross hits the crossbar
thunders doun and crosses the line
Cumnocks supporters erupt
Talbots shut up

the time ticks away
aw the supporters stay
then a wild tackle in the box
results in a penalty kick
and suddenly it's two each

it's unbelievable but it's for real
when the wee winger goes and scores the winner

And we are sailing
Sailing across the water
Stormy water
Just to see you

and the final whistle blaws
and we'll aw be fighting in the streets o Cumnock the night

61

WAN THING
Leonard S. Quinn

Wan thing yi could say aboot Boabby
e croasst a luvly baw. be it
bye-line, shy-line ur coarner poast
wi a big right-back ruffn im up
ur sum hunk ae a centre-hauf
huvin a go at is pins, nivir mind,
wee Boabby slippt roon lik a baur a wet soap
an croasst that baw neat is a sun
risin n settn. settlt thir hash fur thim
oaftin. a tanner baw player mibbe, but
his kinda jookin wis sumthin
wurth lookin it – pally di dance
so it wis. still, e suffert, oh aye
an wee as e wis e wis quick
wi the heid n the boot
an is mitts
scoart oaftin an oaftin.

                     see Boabby but,
tho the wey e wis treatit sa bliddy disgrace,
awlwis e loast the place, sa helluva pity
e croasst the polis. eh?

THE FOOTBALL

Tom Pow

One spring, Dad came home from school
with an old football the gymies
wanted shot of. A real football, mind –

not one of your plastic ones,
but with a teat that sprang up
from the pink bladder, and trembled

between hexagons of rough leather.
Aye, it's a good one that: which is what
he liked to say of anything

that could bear it. Oh and this ball
had seen service! Did they not
kick ones just like it at the Somme?

I stubbed my toes, launching it
into flower beds where it flattened
all it touched. Then when

lamed into the apple trees,
it rained blossom. Banished at last,
I took it to the park with friends

aware of my limitations.
But then other boys came, laughing
up the slope – confident, at ease.

Any game? His ball. *Can we play*?
I sulked on the line as they kicked
the leather off my ball. Later

I carried it home, a stranger's
bloody head, and threw it, clattering,
deep into the shadows of the hut.

THE HALF-TIME DANCER
James Aitchison

Half-time had that brown smell
of pies and bovril and urine
and steamy breath rising
from the big warm beast on the terracing.

An intimate sulphurous smell
of iron and furnaces
clung to the men
even on Saturday afternoons.

And half-time had the march
and countermarch
of bandsmen along the centre line.

Some days the band enticed
out of nowhere
nameless
the dancer, the half-time dancer.

Staring, scared, not daring
to look away, I used to watch
the white-faced thing
flapping about
like a big black stricken bird
down on the cinder track.

I wanted the other men to stop him –
a grown man dancing
and not drunk, not drunk.
The men, without irony,
softly applauded the dancer.

Thirty years later –
dance and dancer
long since lost in the clearances
that swept away
the sulphur and the soft applause –
I know those men were right.

AFTER THE GAME

Maurice Lindsay

He'd never have topped any classes,
or lived to be a shop steward
loud with demand; or bossed masses
figuring promises. He was just
an ordinary boy; somebody's
son who liked football; saw
things fairly, through glasses.

To this day nobody knows
why it should have been him they picked on,
gobbed aim for oaths and spittle
cringed beneath a swell of blows.

At first he pawed circled ground
searching for fairness, dropped sight,
the sweat on animal faces tense
as limping fingers almost found
the broken frame. A kicked-up *shite*
and a cackle crunched both lenses
into the ground. A dustbin clattered ...

Other people mostly stayed
clear, on the other side of the street,
I say ..., one passer-by kept saying,
edged high on helpless conscience.
There was a sound of quickening feet.

A muscular priest punched home
at original sin. The cloth-backed thing
shouldered him out. *Fuck off,
you cuntless prick*, ringing his ears
as he ran to the nearest telephone,
his God too late by countless years.

Meanwhile, the boot went in ... and in ...

There wasn't much the police could do
but the story to the press withheld
the name till they'd told the next-of-kin.

SONG OF THE SUB-WELSHIAN
W. N. Herbert

When A wiz jist a little cunt
ma mither geed me a fuckin dunt
wi a fehv irin
richt oan ma skull
sae A jist laid me doon:
she wiz a punk on junk
she smelt lyk a langdeid skunk,
ma daddy wiz just a drunk
nae tather abaa

    (Chorus of Casuals):
    Nae tather abaa abaa
    O say huv you seen wir baa
    we kicked it richt through yir waa
    nae tather abaa.

When A supported Hibs fur kicks
ma fuckin friends were totally pricks
we shat oan auld wifies
fur livin too near
tae Gorgie Road's surroonds:
as lang as it soonds lik Hell
ye ken it will sell and sell
fur Londoners like thi smell
of a wee bit of rough.

(Chorus):
A wee bit of rough's enough
tae pairt you fae valued stuff
tae protest is to get duffed
by a wee bit of rough.

When A wiz Casual as ye please
A geed thi lassies ma knobby cheese
they sais 'Caa that shaggin?
Take better aim
and don't use the hole that's broon':
hoo lang diz thi Buckfast last?
Hoo fast is a speedfreak's past?
And noo A've assembilt ma cast
nae tather abaa.

(Chorus):
Nae tather abaa abaa
O say can ye see yir baas
we kicked them richt ower that waa
nae tather abaa.

Noo A huv needles of ma ain
and track mark tattoos richt doon ma banes
though E maks me haver
and ravin's inane
A jist write aathin doon:
in a windmill in Amsterdam
A smoke thi pot o thi bam
A'm cream-o-thi-crap-o-grams
A yam whit A yam.

(Chorus):
We yam whit we yam we yam
we think he's King of Siam
wur heids ur filled up wi spam
we yam whut we yam,
whit's Hibee's Hibee
whit's Hibee's Hibee
whit's Hibee's Hibee!

FOOTBALL GOD
Rob Paraman

beneath the rising sun
football god
mister crawford
lays the particles
around the field
when no one's there
to disturb his work
trundling a strange contraption
a funnel on wheels
god knows what it's called
chalk dust
sprinkles through the bottom
inches from the earth
regulation width
icing sugar on the blades of grass
smudging in the mud
white islands in the puddles
wobbling over pot-holes
he lays down the line
separating
game from non-game
in from out
dividing
free kicks from boundary throw-ins
winners from losers
one foot in
one foot out

squeaking as he goes
chalk dust shiva
round the arena
long shadowed
should he leave a gap
the players and umpires
could follow the ball
through
over the fence
play up xavier street
over the train tracks
on and on
ad infinitum

DIRECTIONS

Jim Kay

Was this the way tae Hampden Park,
Glory road tae Scotia's grandeur,
Smooth-surfaced noo the motored asphalt
Buries the ghosts o' clackin' trams
Long gone rattlin' doon Langside,
Bobbed the tammied by the legion,
A surgin' flood tae fill the bowl
Wi' tartan-crested tidal wavers,
Heids a' fair fu' o' expectation
Another Bannockburn tae witness,
Roar on dark blue an' all for Scotland,
A Saturday, sweet April hour,
Sprung fae a drudgin' factory clock,
Ta'en fae a time some work was handy

Aye this is the way tae Hampden Park,
Doon Battlefield Road, sodium lamps
An' clockwork-orangey shop-conversions,
Glitter mask on dyin' stone,
The match reduced, a Wednesday, grey
Wi' decimated city tramps lost in the dark
Deserted terrace, fluorescent shirts
Play oot their farce till mouldifyin'
Crusted pies set in a sea o' puddle piss
Draw doon saft curtain o' the night at last,
On anger-clattered plate-glass sherds
Glimmerin' harsh complex frustrations,
Another self-inflicted Flodden,
The Lowland Clearances wear on

BAG-MEN
Alistair Findlay

Men screamed at Baillie's callused hands, breeze blocks
    rubbing on winter-green,
like having hot ash massaged into concrete thighs –
    'Jock!', you'd say,
'do me first', handing him the liniment, as Baillie came
    between – 'I'll do that, son'.
In twelve seasons, never saw a sponge, a towel and cold
    water in an old lemonade bottle
was all there was, and the threat of them all that was
    needed to have players going down
with broken toes, or ruptured spleens, spring to their feet
    and wave Jock Philiban away,
and his side-kick, old Baillie, clambering from the dug-out.
    'It's alright Jock',
you'd say, 'Where's it hurt son?', and you knew, whether it
    was your eyes or nose or
constipation, as you were saying it, you'd hear a glug, and
    feel your left boot filling up
with cold water, and Baillie rubbing your balls. You'd
    stagger back to your position,
more dazed, with a water-logged foot and an erection: the
    towels round their necks
were for ornament, public display, like the drapes they put
    round coffins at funerals

ANGLOPHOBIA

Hugh McMillan

Sometimes, after ten pints of Pale in Mather's,
my pals and I discuss, with reasoned calm,
the origins of Anglophobia.

The philosophy was mother's milk to me.
Our cat was called Moggy the Bruce.
In 1966 my uncle Billy died on his knees
before the telly screaming 'It didnae
cross the line ye blind bastard!'
I remember my Grandad, seventy five,
and ridged with nicotine, sitting, grimly watching
a schoolgirl's hockey match. Hands like shovels,
he'd never even seen a game with sticks
but he was bawling 'Bully up Fiji,
get intae these English!'

An expression of lost identity, they say.
Some identity.
We were the most manic crew of cutthroats
out, never happy unless we were fighting,
preferably each other; any venue,
Turkestan to Guadeloupe.
It was only after the Pax Britannica
that any of us had a free minute between rounds
to contribute to the culture of the world.

By some strange alchemy we had however found
the untapped source of arrogance and up
to our arses in mud we could thumb our noses
at the Florentines and all the other poofs
of the Renaissance and take some solace
from thumpings by our betters by claiming
moral victory; a piece of turf from Solway
Moss and the crossbar from Culloden.

But despite all that, and sober, the limp
red lions stir the blood and in a crowd of
fellow ba-heids I'll conjure up the pantheon
of Scotland's past and jewel it with lies.
Unswerving stubbornness.
I suppose that in the graveyard of nations
Scotland's epitaph will not be a volume
like the French but a single line:
Ye'll be hearing from us.

THE DAY THAT BRITAIN SPLIT
Robert Alan Jamieson

I was sitting cross-legged,
on the concrete thin carpet,
in front of the outsize Ecko.

Behind me in the red-crimped armchair
Sat the Pole –
Him that lived across the road from Ibrox
In Hinshelwood Drive.

The long spindly legs of the black and white set
Never seemed strong enough to bear
The weight of all that wood, those massive valves.

And bursting from it now, at top volume,
Making it shudder, the World Cup Final 1966.
The War all over again

except that it was only *England* this time.
And the Germans were only 'West'.

Now the speckles dust the monochrome,
Shadowing again
The Hammers – Moore and Martin Peters
And the hat-trick hero, Hurst.

There was never any doubt who he'd support.
The Pole was a sailor who'd played for the ship
with *English* hands
versus international crews,
in all manner of 'away matches',
round the major harbours of the globe –

back then it was
The British Merchant Navy v. the World.

But to me, it was far off 'Inglerun'.
Far from Melby, far from the Huxter Ba.

Why the Pole cheered when *England* won
I understand – they were against the Hun.
Two world wars he'd seen, while I was born too late
To care about 'Commandos',
a Space Age 'Sputnik' bairn.

For me it took a year to care,
At Wembley, when McCalliog scored
And listening to the wireless
I swallowed my PK chewing gum,
Jumping up and down in joy.

In boxing terms, that made us Scottish champions
beating champions, like
But only in boxing terms.

DADDY EDGAR'S POOLS

Mike Harding

Each week you, Thursday Millionaire, would conjure up
The ju-ju, stab the coupon with a pin
Or read the cups, perm my age and height
With Hitler's birthday and the number of
The bus that passed the window and the clump
Of pigeons on the next door neighbour's loft.

With rabbit's foot, white heather, and wishbone
You fluenced the coupon that I ran to post.

Each muggy Saturday you sat still while the set
Called out into the hushed room where I sat
With burning ears and heard a London voice
Call names as strange as shipping forecasts through the air:
Hamilton Academicals, Queen of the South,
Pontefract United, Hearts of Midlothian,
Wolverhampton Wanderers, Arbroath, Hibernian,
And once, I thought, a boy called *Patrick Thistle.*

Then every week after the final check,
When Friday's dreams were scratched out with a squeaky pen,
You took down from upstairs your brass band coat,
Gave me the wad of polish and the button stick.
And there in that still, darkened room I polished up
Each brassy button world that showed my face;
While you on shining tenor horn played out
Your Thursday Millionaire's lament
For a poor man's Saturday gone.

FOOTBALL HAIKUS
Lorna Waite

Equality before goal

Bruce	Burns	Baxter
Quine	McQueen	Country

Scots wha play
That nation again
Kilts worn here
Thistles unite sections
Scottish nation, defend
Thesis antithesis result

POLITICS
Border guards goalie
Goalmouth sanctuary seekers
Left Wing Surge

SURREALISM
Jimmy sees hats
Hemp den score

CONCEPTUAL ART
Still white line
Filling empty space

SCOTTISH HISTORY PLAY
Towsy toerag tackle
Beautiful miss Scotland
Skinklin saltire shimmie
Refs rob roy
Curl hurl burl
Final score settled

Equality after goal

THE OLDEST GAME
(*from Men on Ice*)
Andrew Greig

Ah, the assent of women, sighed Poet,
Why don't you blunt your edge there, Axe-Man?
So Axe explained as night
slid over the ice.

Ma break came when I wis playing around
wi' the lads   we'd heard there was someone
looking fer talent   I made a few smairt moves
I've aye had style tae ma brut

    so she signed me up
    Put It There she said
    so I did

And in time made her first eleven
an' made ma climb tae fame
putting it in from a' ways
in the heat of the moment nin faster

    there wis animal roar
    when I wis on the ba'
    jist watching the replay
    wud knacker ye

There wis some talk
o' long-term contract aye but
ye canna believe a'thing ye hear
in this game   lemme jist say

      it's magick
      when you're big
      when you're Up There

Great till wan afternoon I went in
low and hard frae behind
aw I wis provoked ref
the wee black book for me

Frae then on I wis nowhere
tried too hard   lost the timing
running a' over the park
niver where the action wis

      time I got there
      it had moved on   I
      couldna get tae the ba'

Na, the ba' game is fer mugs
tae mony folk after the wan thing
gimme the moonless nights
gimme ma axe

      I play my ain game
      agin the boys in navy blue
      watch ma style

GIRL FOOTBALLER
Jackie Kay

The ball soars and the ball flies.
The ball goes up. The ball goes in.
And the balls in your eyes,
are rolling and spinning,
spinning and rolling.
And the blood in your heart is singing.

You feel yourself whirl and twirl.
What a talented girl.
Nothing like this feeling you get
when the ball bulges in the back of the net.
No, you don't easily forget
the sweet sweet taste of a goal.
Replay it in your mind again:

Left foot in the air, flick,
straight to the back of the net.
Play it again and again
– the ball's beautiful roll to the goal.
Nothing like the soaring and roaring
when the plump ball hits the thin net.
And the sad blue goalie sits on the sad green grass.
The look on the slow face,
watching the ball go past, fast.
No chance. No chance. Watching the ball dance.
You dribble from the midfield down.
You get past three men.
You do a chip, a volley, you curl the ball.
You perm the air with your talent, and all
the fans sizzle and spark,
all the fans sing and dance,
football is one long romance
with the ball, with the ball and all.

You nutmeg the goalie like the goalie is a spice.
You get the ball in, not once, twice, but thrice!
Hat trick! You make the goalie feel sick.
So lie you down and roll in celebration.
You feel the team jump up on your back
Then you feel the whole nation,
Goggle-eyed in admiration.
You squeeze your fist,
Like this, like a kiss, to the wild crowd
And your football of a heart
is bouncing and proud.

75

THE BLUES
Lilian Anderson

He was owre mauchtless
ti gang til the gemme,
sae he sklentit alane
at the television
wi a roll up an a lager;
Glesca Rangers, The licht blues
they did mair for him
nor ony psychiatrist

76

SCOTTISH LEAGUE CUP FINAL, 1959
Hearts 2 – Third Lanark 1
Anonymous

In days of old, when Hearts were bold, and Begbie led them out,
So says the tale, the West turned pale, to hear the Gorgie shout,
When down the wing, young Baird would swing, up went a
    thund'rous roar,
And with the cry, the hats went high, when Michael dashed to score,
Or Bobby Walker shone in the fight with deft deceptive glide,
Now to attack, or else fall back, the foe could not decide,
Now to reclaim the old time fame, the Gorgie Lion hail!
Hist! Hear it growl, out on the prowl, a-lashing of its tail,
Prey? Any kind! – he doesn't mind, just this he would confide,
Above the rest, he'd like it best, frae Glesca on the Clyde!

77

I. M. DAVIE COOPER,
d. March 95
Angus Calder

Beats one beats two beats three beats four beats five –
that Davie Cooper feints and glides and jinks.
The ranks of Jambos can't forbear to cheer
though it's against them, this sweet goal he sinks

when driving almost to the line, he pots
at a fifteen-degree angle. Henry Smith
the goalie can do nothing. Tynecastle erupts
and Davie Cooper dances into myth.

The best of all, Rude Gullit said – he'd know.
Pele said that of Best, so aptly named,
Best let his gift die: Davie's really dead.
Aged 39, Gods loved him, he was claimed.

I dread that you, my love, might be so sudden.
Beauty like yours, envied by Aphrodite,
Pallas Athene might decide to clutch
up to the starscape, soaring past the flighty,

the lipsticked and the perfumed and mascaraed
uncertain and confused poor women, those
who substitute cosmetics for directness,
nudge intellect to smalltalk, sex to pose.

Davie at his best was like our dawn in bed
when time's away and somewhere else. We move
as if defences don't exist except
as shadows of the excellence we prove.

In fact, there's no defence, there's no attack –
pure compliance, as if Smith in goal
had summoned Davie to his line, as if
Hearts needed Cooper to make fortune whole.

Sandy, beside me then, denies it now,
says that he didn't will that Rangers score,
but he did, I did, everyone there did.
Now Scotland mourns that we will see no more

like that, like Coop, that selfsame excellence,
handsome and strict, his own man, wouldn't go
to England, Europe even, so Clydebank
and Motherwell and Ibrox know they owe

a grieving in return. Like perfect love
when best is given, nothing but the best
should be riposted. After so much bad faith,
such wrong turns, it's with you I've come to rest

I hope. Though Siegfried didn't. Down the Rhine
he came to be betrayed. And served him right –
crude hero, he had none of Davie's polish:
whereas your star would ornament the night

and when I hear you playing Siegfied's horn
all heroism's purged, there's no bad faith
possible, just for that time, at all,
ever again. I watch now Davie's wraith

dance excellently through the dazzled shades
of all the hard full backs, the cynic foulers –
beauty and innocence and honesty
as in the movements of midsummer bowlers

at evening on the quiet green, old men and women
at ease with quiet pleasure, slowly proving
that the Gods may love those who die old
as we might darling, still replete with loving.

IN THE BILL NICHOLSON SUITE[1]

Sarah Wardle

This football is a found poem.
On it Danny Blanchflower signed
the names of his winning team,
when Tottenham Hotspur completed
the Double in '61. Here are the scorers,
Smith and Dyson, and the score:
Spurs 2, Leicester City 0. And there
Bill Nicholson autographed the back
on leather the colour of faded parchment.

This football is a testament of victory,
an historical document, witness
to an age of meritocracy.
These are not the names
of hereditary kings, but of men
who succeeded and deserved to win.

This football sits in a glass case,
as if it's been kicked
straight out of the past. But this
is not relic, no museum piece.
See. This football is still in use,
staring back like an idol's head,
still worshipped now as much as then.

[1] see Introduction re John White

from THE VISITOR

D. M. Black

We
kick the
small bean-tin into the gutter. Someone
dribbles it adroitly out. From the café an
aged man applauds. For every three of us there is a
light can, that we
set and tackle for. Half the village is
cheering from the pavement. We

go into the café. Beer: it is
on the house. Laughter and talking.

80

FI'BAW IN THE STREET
Robert Garioch

Shote! here's the poliss,
the Gayfield poliss,
    an thull pi'iz in the nick fir
    pleyan fi'baw in the street!
Yin o' thum's a faw'y
like a muckle foazie taw'y,
    bi' the ither's lang and skinnylike,
    wi umbrelly feet.
Ach, awaw, says Tammy Curtis,
fir thir baith owre blate ti hurt iz,
    thir a glaikit pair o Teuchters
    an as Heilant as a peat.
Shote! thayr thir comin
wi the hurdy-gurdy wummin
    tha' we coupit wi her puggy
    pleyan fi'baw in the street.

faw'y: fatty; *foazie taw'y*: soft tattie; *blate*: feart

Sae wir aff by Cockie-Dudgeons an
　　the Sandies and the Coup,
and wir owre a dizzen fences tha'
　　the coppers canny loup,
and wir in an ou' o back greens an
　　wir dreepan muckel dikes,
an we tear ir claes on railins
　　full o nesty irin spikes.
An aw the time the skinnylinky
　　copper's a' ir heels,
though the faw'y's deid ir deean,
　　this yin seems ti rin on wheels:
noo he's stickit on a railin wi
　　his helmet on a spike,
noo he's up an owre an rinnan, did
　　ye iver see the like?

Bi' we stour awa ti Puddocky
　　(that's doon by Logie Green)
and wir roon by Beaverhaw whayr
　　deil a beaver's iver seen;
noo wir aff wi' buitts and stockins
　　and wir wadin roon a fence
(i' sticks oot inty the wa'er, bi'
　　tha's nithin if ye've sense)
syne we cooshy doon thegither
　　jist like chookies wi a hen
in a bonny wee-bit bunky-hole
　　tha' bobbies dinny ken.
Bi' ma knees is skint and bluddan,
　　an ma breeks they want the seat,
jings! ye git mair nir ye're eftir,
　　playan fi'baw in the street.

GREEN PAIRK DAYS
Raymond Vettese

Quick slim creator o perfect passes,
needle threidin onie defence,
wi a hat-trick against Ferryden Strollers,
a salmon-lowp heider in the final meenit
whan the Bridge Street Boys seemed shair o twa points.
Legend amang us, Ginger Jones,
jinkin doon the richt wing in the Green Pairk Days.

I met him juist the ither week
and an auld begrutten story wis telt;
he wis oot o wark, hoastie, reid-fat wi booze.
Och the baa's birst wis aa he could tackle
whan I blethart aboot the Green Pairk Days,
the baa's birst. I kent whit he meant,
an' bocht him a nip afore he hirpelt awa.

DO' CARE

Bashabi Fraser

In a Paris hotel lounge on one occasion
My thirteen-year-old five-foot-five
Daughter glowed with the attention
Of three young men striving
To pigeon-hole her Scottishness
And break her brittle brusqueness
With their far-eastern finesse.

If Scotland played England
Whom would she support
– Sco'land – was the answer delivered
And if England played India
– India – she claimed with triumphant swagger.
If England played Germany
– Germany was the response
From the unassailable position
Of a new-found nationalism.

And what if it were Scotland and India
One demanded with the diabolical confidence
Of an argument-winning lawyer –
She clamped down her glass, shrugged her bare
Shoulders, turned away saying – do' care.

WORLD CUP SUMMER
Julia Darling

Gawky. Eight. She stares
at a fright of magpie[1] strips
flapping towards her.

Come on LADS!

thunders coach,
a man whose tea is now baking.
She shrugs, attempting indifference,
lopes to his whistle.

Come ON lads!
Pace. PACE.
Tuck in behind him.
Worry him.

Coach is FIFA, I am Big Jack,
agitated beyond the white line,
longing to run to her
with water.

---

[1] *magpie*, nickname for Newcastle United FC's black and white strip

DON'T JUST STAND THERE, TACKLE!

If football is theatre,
don't let my girl be an understudy.
Coach doesn't hear.
He has made her a sub,
practising skills on the sideline,

and at night she will paste
footballer's shaven faces
into her scrapbook,
dreaming of shinpads.

Oh god of football and improbability,
let Ireland win the World Cup.

And let her keep a foothold
on this uneven pitch.

MATCH OF THE DAY
Ken Morrice

A nation maun hack oot its destiny,
heist it heich and gar it glister.

But aye there's dowie echoes:
the skirl o pipes, the beat o drums,
mindin us o bluid-rin battles,
fechts that planked us on oor bums.

Destiny for Scots is a muckle steen
far kings langsyne got crooned.
Aye keekin hindwards, we swither,
and slaik the wairsh auld wounds.

But noo at lest the nation stirs,
ettlin tae coup the Sassenach hurly,
getting yokit tae its ain weird and nae
bamboozled by politicians' whurlie-burlie.

'The natives are restless,' Carruthers girns,
gawpin North at soond o drums.
'Flowers of Scotland, by George! Burns
and Wallace next, and marching South
no doubt demanding nationhood and freedom.'

heich: high; *dowie*: dismal; *weird*: destiny

'Freedom and whisky gang thegither,'
quo Alick, jist tae lats aa ken.
'A wee hauf, gin ye please, Nellie,
afore the missus gangs fair gyte –
for I was expecked hame yestreen.
But tell's, fit time's the match on the telly?'

gin: if; *gyte:* mental

85

EURO 96: A FAN'S FAREWELL

John Burnside

Like all those red-faced boys
in brand new football strips

dribbling a ball around
in a circle of streetlight

or practicing their footwork
in the park

in Cowdenbeath, Arbroath,
Kircudbright, Govan,

I wanted the triumph of willpower
over strength

grace over
money

and stood with my head in my hands
for the longest time

when we missed
that goal,

still blaming no one, hopeful
to the last,

aware of how often, in life,
the impossible happens.

PITTODRIE WINTER, 4.45PM
Tom Bryan

Grass under shellac of ice,
ball skites wide,
always out of touch.
Sky oily black
while European memories
float from floodlit haze.

Brown puddles form where a man could drown,
one last chance is knocked to touch,
cold rain keeps falling down.

FOOTBALL! FOOTBALL! FOOTBALL!
Sean O'Brien

My sporting life (may I refer to me?)
Was never all it was supposed to be.
Mine was a case of talent unfulfilled.
I blame society, which blames my build.

From trap and pass and backheel in the yard
To deskbound middle age is something hard
For the Eusebio of '64
To grasp: you don't play football any more.

Your boots and kit are all gone into dust
And your electric pace a thing of rust.
Whatever knocks the football fates inflict
On Shearer now, your chance of being picked

If England reach the *Mondiale* in France
(Does Umbro really make that size of pants?)
Is smaller than the risk of being brained
By frozen urine falling from a plane,

And though you'll stop by any rainy park
To watch folks kick a ball until its dark
You don't expect Dalglish will seek you out
To ask you what the game is all about.

But more fool him, you secretly suspect:
You've seen the lot, from Crewe to Anderlecht,
From Gornik to Stranraer to River Plate.
The Cosmos and Montrose and Grampus Eight,

From Accies, Bochum, Galatasaray,
Finbogdottir, Dukla Prague (away),
Botafogo, Bury, Reggiana …
Football! Football! Football! Work? *Mañana*.

Sponsored by IKEA and by Andrex,
Butch in sacks or mincing on in Spandex,
The great, the mediocre, the pathetic,
Real Madrid and Raggy-Arse Athletic –

Twelve quid a week or fifty grand an hour,
The game retains the undiminished power
To stop the clock, accelerate the blood
And sort the decent geezer from the crud.

From 5–3–2 to Kaiser Franz libero
Is there a team formation you don't know?
Experience! There is no substitute
For working out why Andy Cole can't shoot.

The fields of dream and nightmare where the great
Line up beside the donkeys to debate
Who gets the league, the cup, the bird, the chop
And whether Coventry deserve the drop

Are graveyards of a century's desire
To keep the youth that sets the world on fire –
Pele's '58, Diego's '86,
And Pushkas hushing Wembley with his tricks …

And back and back to James and Meredith
And all the tricky Welsh who took the pith,
Until West Auckland marmalize Juventus –
World on world through which the game has sent us,

Until at last we stand in some back lane
You're Cantona but I'll be Best again.
Who gives a toss what any of it means
While there are Platinis and Dixie Deans

And life is always Saturday, from three
Till *Sports Report*, as it's supposed to be,
The terrace in its shroud of freezing breath,
Hot leg, crap ref, a soft goal at the death,

Fags and Bovril, bus home, bacon sandwich –
Paradise in anybody's language
Is listening for the fate of Stenhousemuir
(Robbed by Brechin 27–4).

5–A–SIDES

(*Bathgate Sports Centre*)

Alistair Findlay

Twang! Hammy's ham-string goes again as he's taking aff
    his jaicket, Wee Rab,
stripped to the waist, Bathgate's Little Buddah, four big
    cheeks, two quick feet
and no much hair left, but a great player nanetheless, ex-
    Dunfermline, excessive
in onythin fae eatin pies tae drinkin tae fightin weemin aff,
    aye Rab, in yer dreams!
Wee Jock, a human dynamo, Mojo, on a go-slow, the
    Flying Finn, ah, here's a trick!
nah, hear that click? his knee's gaun, and he's gaun doon
    himsel, in instalments,
like aw the rest; Dugan, 'the ba's mine', Colin, an enigma,
    a riddle of the Sphinx,
sometimes brilliant, sometimes stinks, mince combined
    with grace;
Airthur, a heid-case, always complainin aboot the kitty
    and him no gettin oany,
drink that is, but a major singer; Wee Tam, a whiz-bang,
    for whom fitba is wan
lang whang, an endless skid; then there's the kid himsel,
    Big Eamon, frae Dublin,
which is where his tackles begin; Eck Mathieson, gone
    but not forgiven;

Big Tam, a cultured left foot if things are going great but
    can vibrate if you are not
pulling your own weight; Faggot, a mistake, broke his leg
    tripping ower his ain feet;
then there's masel, the bringer of the ball, ex-mair clubs
    than Jack Nicholas:
and Sudsie – what can you say? Sudsie's just, Sudsie's
    just, well, wi' Sudsie, words just fail.

SATURDAY NIGHT
Stephen Scobie

Saturday night was when my father worked:
no time of relaxation, the centre of his week.
He sat in his study, transferring his beliefs
into the wise and simple words of his sermons.

Around 10.30 he might come downstairs,
drink tea, eat toast and marmalade, and watch
TV replays of the afternoon's games;
and then return to his desk and blue-covered notebooks.

For forty years he followed this good discipline:
and when he preached, the congregation listened
to the words of a friend they had known at times
when life did things they could not understand.

An hour or so ago I came home from a movie:
the house was quiet, the TV doesn't show Queen's Park.
I sit in my study thinking of my father,
writing this poem late on Saturday night.

90

from **Tàladh Dhòmhnaill Ghuirm**

Anonymous c. 1650

Le a mhuime

Nàile bho hì nàile bho h-àrd
Nàile bho hì nàile bho h-àrd
Ar leam gur h-ì   a'ghrian 's i ag éirigh
Nàile bho h-àrd   's i a' cur small
Nàile bho h-ì air na reultaibh.

nàile ri triall *hò*
Gu cùirt Dhòmhnaill   nan sgiath ballbhreac
Nan lann ceanngheal   nan saighead siùbhlach
Nan long seòlach   nam fear meanmnach.

Hó nàile nàile nàile le chéile
Ge bè àite   an tàmh thu an Alba
Bidh sud mar ghnàths abb   ceòl is seanchas
Pìob is clàrsach   àbhachd 's dannsa
Bidh cairt uisge   suas air phlanga,
Ol fiona is   beòir ad champa
Is gur lìonmhor triubhas   saoithreach seang ann.

Nàile nàile   *nàile hó nàile*
An uair théid mac *hó*   mor rìgh-sa deiseil
Chan ann air chóignear   chan ann air sheisear
Chann ann air naoinear   chan ann air dheichnear
Ceud 'nan suidhe leat   ceud 'nan seasamh leat.

Ceud eile, *hó*, bhith cur   a' chupa deiseal dhut
Dà cheud deug bhith   dèanamh chleasa leat
Dà cheud deug bhith   cur a' bhuill-choise leat
Da cheud deug bhith   'n òrdugh gleaca leat.

from DONALD GORM'S LULLABY
(translation)
Anonymous c. 1650

By His Nurse

Naile from-Iona, Naile from above,
Naile from Iona, Naile from above,
I think that it is   the sun as it rises
Naile from above   that is casting a haze
Naile from Iona   over the stars.

Naile Naile Naile traveling *ho*
to the court of Donald   of the studded targes,
of the swords bright-pointed,   of the flying arrows,
of the many-sailed birlins,   of the spirited clansmen.

Ho Naile Naile Naile together,
whatever the place you   stay in Scotland
this will be usual: music and talking,
piping and harping,   mirth and dancing,
quarts of whisky   up on the table,
drinking of wine and   beer in encampment,
and many pairs of breeches   tight and well-fashioned.

Naile Naile
when the son of
it isn't with five men,
it isn't with nine men,
but one hundred with you sitting,

Naile *ho* Naile
my King travels southwards
it isn't with six men,
it isn't with ten men,
one hundred standing.

A hundred sending
twelve hundred others
twelve hundred driving
twelve hundred standing

sunwise the cup to you,
to frisk and sport with you,
the football across to you,
in battle array with you.

[verses 1, 2, 5–7]

4 FOOTBALL HAIKU
Tom Leonard

Bovril Zen

hawf time
n wan hawn clappin
whair the fuck um ah

auld an firm

a blue sky
a green grunn
an a bowl a hatred

playground football

a hawnfu a boays
n two jaickits
three an in

this sporting life

doon three wan
a rid raw wind
nthi ref a bastard

STAIRWAY

Andrew McGeever

Strong shipyard cranes suspend a Govan sky:
it's afternoon, yet floodlights pierce the dark.
Processions of fans as far as the eye
can see: it's the Ne'erday match at Ibrox Park.
No ordinary Saturday: the blue
and green collide again to weave designs
of Old Firm passion. Tramping feet of true
supporters fashion drumbeats, loud and fine.
The full-time score sees honours even. Wait;
tread gently down those terrace stairs, hold tight
to hands and railings, reach the exit gate.
Get home and tell the family you're all right.
Sixty-six bodies gasp in vain for breath
as football buckles under the weight of death.

'RESERVE-ATIONS'
(*the number 12's lament*)
John McGilvray

They put a shirt upon my back,
And sling me shorts too tight or slack,
Socks with holes in toe and heel,
How the hell do you think I feel.

Last to leave the dressing room,
Carry flags, I must assume,
Plus water bucket, first aid kit,
Just the thing to make me fit.

Reach the pitch and run the line,
Five minutes more until half-time,
Cut the oranges, hand them out,
This is what it's all about.

Wave my hankie, feeling fine,
Hoping for the skipper's sign,
Minutes left, he calls my name,
Glory be! I've got a game!

Run and stumble, slowly fall,
Forget about the bloody ball!
Writhing on the green, green grass,
Feeling foolish on my 'ass' –

Carried off with twisted knee,
Bloody great! it would be me,
Game has ended – 'Hard luck sub,
See you at the nearest pub.'

Drowning sorrow, downing beer,
Pessimistic now I fear,
Next week's team? Wait and see.
I bet you number 12 is me.

NIL NIL

Don Paterson

*Just as any truly accurate representation of a particular
geography can only exist on a scale of 1:1 (imagine the
vast, rustling map of Burgundy, say, settling over it
like a freshly-starched sheet!) so it is with all our
abandoned histories, those ignoble lines of succession
that end in neither triumph nor disaster, but merely
plunge on into deeper and deeper obscurity; only in
the infinite ghost-libraries of the imagination – their
only possible analogue – can their ends be pursued,
the dull and terrible facts finally authenticated.*
                                    Francois Aussemain, *Pensees*

From the top, then, the zenith, the silent footage:
McCrandle, majestic in ankle-length shorts,
his golden hair shorn to an open book, sprinting
the length of the park for the long hoick forward,
his balletic toe-poke nearly bursting the roof
of the net; a shaky pan to the Erskine St End
where a plague of grey bonnets falls out of the clouds.
But ours is a game of two halves, and this game
the semi they went on to lose; from here
it's all down, from the First to the foot of the Second,
McGrandle, Visocchi and Spankie detaching
like bubbles to speed the descent into pitch-sharing,
pay-cuts, pawned silver, the Highland Division,
the absolute sitters ballooned over open goals,
the dismal nutmegs, the scores so obscene

no respectable journal will print them; though one day
Farquhar's spectacular bicycle-kick
will earn him a name-check in Monday's obituaries.
Besides the one setback – the spell of giant-killing
in the Cup (Lochee Violet, then Aberdeen Bon Accord,
the deadlock with Lochee Harp finally broken
by Farquhar's own-goal in the replay)
nothing inhibits the 50-year slide
into Sunday League, big tartan flasks,
open hatchbacks parked squint behind goal-nets,
the half-time satsuma, the dog on the pitch,
then the Boy's Club, sponsored by Skelly Assurance,
then Skelly Dry Cleaners, then nobody;
stud-harrowed pitches with one-in-five inclines,
grim fathers and perverts with Old English Sheepdogs
lining the touch, moaning softly.
Now the unrefereed thirty-a-sides,
terrified fat boys with calipers minding
four jackets on infinite, notional fields;
ten years of dwindling, half-hearted kickabouts
leaves two little boys – Alastair Watt,
who answers to 'forty', and wee Horace Madden,
so smelly the air seems to quiver above him –
playing desperate two-touch with a bald tennis ball
in the hour before lighting-up time.
Alastair cheats, and goes off with the ball
leaving wee Horace to hack up a stone
and dribble it home in the rain;
past the stopped swings, the dead shanty-town
of allotments, the black shell of Skelly Dry Cleaners
and into his cul-du-sac, where, accidentally,
he neatly back-heels it straight into the gutter
then tries to swank off like he meant it.

Unknown to him, it is all that remains
of a lone fighter-pilot, who, returning at dawn
to find Leuchars was not where he'd left it,
took time out to watch the Sidlaws unsheathed
from their great black tarpaulin, the haar burn off Tayport
and Venus melt into Carnoustie, igniting
the shoreline; no wind, not a cloud in the sky
and no one around to admire the discretion
of his unscheduled exit: the engine plopped out
and would not re-engage, sending him silently
twirling away like an ash-key,
his attempt to bail out only partly successful,
yesterday having been April the 1st –
the ripcord unleashing a flurry of socks
like a sackful of doves rendered up to the heavens
in private irenicon. He caught up with the plane
on the ground, just at the same instant the tank blew
and made nothing of him, save for his fillings,
his tickets, his lucky half-crown and his gallstone,
now anchored between the steel bars of a stank
that looks to be biting the bullet on this one.

In short, this is where you get off, reader;
I'll continue alone, on foot, in the fading light,
following the trail as it steadily fades
into road-repairs, birdsong, the weather, nirvana,
the plot thinning down to a point so refined
not even the angels could dance on it. Goodbye.

DENIS LAW
Parry Maguire

The natural freedom
Whose wise limbs
Came to life
As the King who reigned
Over defences with his fingers
Digging deep into sleeve-ends
The skinny frame
Quicker than a cat on heat
Twisting like spaghetti
Wrapped around a fork.

SOMEWHERE ON THE SOUTH CHINA SEA IN 1938

Ian McMillan

The waves rose and fell like the Lanarkshire hills;
My dad stood on the deck of a ship that pitched
And rolled and thought of Cathkin Park.

Not perfectly flat, but flatter than this.

His dad had told him by his joiner's bench
Of the Argentinian tour the team undertook
Via Cherbourg, Coruna, Vigo and Lisbon in 1923.

Not a perfect year, but better than some.

And maybe that made the link: Third Lanark/
Romance/World Travel/ and my dad
Signed up for the navy and the endless horizons.

Not a perfect job, but sweeter than many.

And nobody knew how things would turn out:
The war, the future, the long decline of a club
Until the last ball kicked, the last whistle blown;

Not a perfect end, and sadder than most.

But now my dad gazes out at some flying fish
Beautifully low over the South China water, carving the space,
Like Third Lanark on a perfect Saturday

Yes, perfect. Just perfect. Cathkin Park perfect.

THE ENTRY OF SHANKLY INTO LIVERPOOL

Parry Maguire

From Huddersfield
Driving down in an Austin A40
No palms were thrown at his feet
No sweet Hosannas filled the skies
No heralds announced the saviour's arrival
And beneath Liverpool's sullen grey skies
He walked, the anointed one, in his Jimmy Cagney suit
Football boots in one hand
Football's soul in the other.

ECHALER

Ian Stephen

Tool handles seasoning in the flow,
wet wood wearing white as a hand-palm.
Plain stones as weights on red clay eaves:
the Sirocco winds travel this far.

Now the geraniums are silent,
bedded outdoors in painted churns.
Car-parts occupy the blacksmith's window,
behind wrought work of Basque crosses.

We walk by without a peseta's worth of
either of their languages: apart until,
in a concrete court, the known and fast
declensions of the grammar of soccer.

FITBA CLICHÉ
(*the ba's no for eatin*)
Alistair Findlay

I remember being told by big MacIntyre
tae take mair time oan the ba. Listen, son, he says,
ye're playin like the gress wis oan fire,
Yer blindin us a' wi' the stour.

This is a gemm fur men,
no boays, or weans, or jessies.
If yer good enough, yer big enough, they say,
but, never listen or play tae the crowd,
an' forget a' yer faither's advice,
an' yer great-uncle Tam's an a',
whae played wi' Champfleurie Violet's Cup Winning Team.
They days are a' gaun, like snaw aff
a Geordie Young clearance.

Then
it wis the people's gemm,
a' aboot the ba', an beatin' yer men,
this way then that, then swingin it ower frae the wing,
an up like a bird tae heid it awa' an intae the net.
The goalie, auld as yer faither an dressed like yer granny,
stuck in the mud like a big stranded whale, Goal!
And a hundred thousand voices sang in Hampden Park.
Ye couldnae see the sun fur bunnets.

Romantic?
Aye! And a' for the glory o' it.
Well, that's a' shite noo son,
the ba's no for eatin' oanie mair.

Time was
when ye could tell a prospect
by the way he shed his hair,
or jouked by his relations in the scullery,
but, we still believed in Empire then,
ken,
when the Wee Blue Devils buried themsels at the England End,
and half o' Europe, for a glory that wisnae worth haen,
oor ain, singin and deein like cattle,
brought hame not one lullaby in gaelic.

In the room the punters come and go
Talking of Di Stephano

On the terraces,
beneath the stand,
a poet speaks for a nation:

the ref's a baam.

We,
whaur the comic and the cosmic meet,
an ambulance ball, a crowded street,
a psyche and a jersey steeped ower dark
b'the ruck, a people still, unique,
manoeuvrin, multiform and chic, aye missus,
chic as fuck.

SCOT-LAND! SCOT-LAND! SCOTLAND!

Scotland,
turn yir backs tae the grandstand,
forget the suicide ba',
think mair o keepin' possession,
Christ, frae some o yer ain side ana',

Listen.
Ye cannae play fitba' withoot the ba', okay?
An ye cannae govern yerself without a country,
even if ye are oan the committee.
(England taught us that)

Right then,

Play wir ain gemme,
Afore the ba' eats *us*.

Again!

GLASGOW 2015

James Robertson

Returning from Glasgow after years out of touch,
Nothing at first seemed changed very much.
But then at the STV centre I found
A clanjamfrie of citizens milling around
Electronic billboards flashed messages there –
" 'LIVE PHILOSOPHY' pays for minority fare
Game Show" – this and others transmitted anew
In Scots and in Gaelic, Chinese and Urdu.
"We announce the repeat of the popular series
On MacFadyen (the Younger)'s 'Low Energy' theories –
To be followed by this year's Saint Andrew's Night Thesis
By Seamus MacIomhair, retiring as preses
Of the 'Front de la Prètique Geophysique' ..."
I stared at such marvels, unable to speak
Or to credit the latest of these progress shocks –
"SPORTS EXTRA: first Scotswoman signed at Ibrox!"

NOTES

1   **ALEXANDER SCOTT** was born in Aberdeen (1920–1989); his studies at Aberdeen University were interrupted by the War, during which he was awarded the MC for distinguished services with the Gordon Highlanders; a lecturer at Edinburgh and Glasgow Universities where he established the first (and still only) Department of Scottish Literature and served as its Head until he retired; academic, poet, literary biographer – notably of William Soutar, *Still Life* (London, 1958) – editor of *Akros* and anthologies with Norman MacCaig and Michael Grieve, he actively promoted Scottish literature in schools and universities; *Collected Poems: 1920–1990,* ed David S. Ross.

2   **ANONYMOUS C. 1580**

3   **HUGH MACDIARMID**, born Christopher Murray Grieve in Langholm, Dumfriesshire (1892–1978); never completed training to be a teacher in Edinburgh, worked as a journalist in Scotland and Wales, served in the RAMC during the Great War; edited *Northern Numbers*, 1920–22, and a periodical *Scottish Numbers*, through which he launched the modernist Scots lyrics of 'Hugh MacDiarmid' whose *A Drunk Man Looks at the Thistle* (1926) galvanised the Scottish Literary Renaissance movement; controversial and provocative, he joined the Communist Party and helped found the National Party of Scotland, being expelled from both, and re-joining both; properly regarded as the towering figure of 20th century Scottish literature; *The Complete Poems of Hugh MacDiarmid*, two volumes (1978, 1985).

4   **DEREK BOWMAN** was born in Liverpool (1931–1987), where he lived until his early 20s; after National Service he taught Modern Languages in Germany and England, becoming a lecturer in German at Edinburgh University in 1964; widely published in

Scots literary magazines – *Lines Review, Chapman, Akros, Words, Cencrastus* – as a poet and reviewer until his death in 1987; published two books – a translation of Ulrick Brakers *The Poor Man of Toggenberg* (Edinburgh, 1970) and *Life into Autobiography: A Study of Goethe's 'Dichtung und Wahrhect'* (Bern, 1971); appeared alongside Liz Lochhead, Andrew Greig and Brian McCabe in *Seven New Voices*, ed John Schofield, Garret Arts, Edinburgh, 1972 and *Made in Scotland: An Anthology of 14 Scottish Poets*, ed Robert Garioch, Carcanet Press, 1974.

5   **TOM LEONARD** was born in Glasgow in 1944; educated at Glasgow University; his *Collected Poems* 1965–2004 comprise his seminal *Intimate Voices: Selected Work* 1965–83 and *access to the silence: poems* 1984–2004; essays and criticism collected in *Reports from the Present* (1995); an anthology, *Radical Renfrew: Poetry from the French Revolution to the First World War* (1989); a biography, *Places of the Mind: The Life and Work of James Thomson (BV)*; works part-time as Professor of Creative Writing at the University of Glasgow, and his website is www.tomleonard.co.uk

6   **RAYMOND FRIEL** was born in Greenock in 1963; educated at Glasgow University, moved to England where he trained as a teacher; lives with his wife and three sons in Somerset; works as a headteacher of a secondary school in Bath; co-edited the review *Southfields* and ran Southfields Press for a number of years; collections include *Bel-Air* (1993), *Seeing the River* (1995), *Renfrewshire in Old Photographs* (2000), *A World Fit to Live in* (2005).

7   **BRIAN MCCABE** was born in a mining village near Edinburgh, where he now lives; educated at Edinburgh University and a full-time writer since 1980; various residencies and fellowships, including the William Soutar Fellowship in Perth;

appointed Writer in Residence at Edinburgh University in 2005; award winning author of three poetry collections, three short-story collections and two novels; *Spring's Witch* (1984), *One Atom to Another* (1987), *Body Parts* (Canongate, 1999).

8   **LIZ NIVEN** was born in Glasgow in 1952; educated at Glasgow University and Jordanhill College of Education; a teacher for 10 years in Easter Ross and 18 years in Newton Stewart, Galloway, she has been Scots Language Development Officer for Dumfries and Galloway and Writer-in-Residence for Dumfries and Galloway Arts Association; worked in collaboration with sculptors and wood-carvers along the River Cree in Galloway; recent collections include *Cree Lines* (2000), *Stravaigin* (Luath, 2006) and *Burning Whins and Other Poems* (Luath, 2004).

9   **DEREK ROSS** was born in Stranraer in 1956 which he left in 1973 to work in the Microbiology Department at Dumfries and Galloway Royal Infirmary where he is a Senior Medical Scientist; a photographer, he has held joint poetry/photography exhibitions with Angus MacMillan – *Canan's Solus* (2003), *Tidelines* (2004), *Beyond the Walls* (2005); his poems have appeared in literary Scots literary magazines and anthologies and in *Origins, Volume* 10, (Markings Publications, Kirkcudbright, 1997); he was one of the Museum of Scotland's 'Present Poets'.

10   **JANET PAISLEY** was born in Ilford, Essex in 1948 and raised in Avonbridge, a village near Falkirk, in which area she raised her seven sons, one of whom died, as a single parent after her divorce; multi-award winning poet, playwright, writer of fiction, non-fiction, radio, television and screen who also writes for children; won Britain's biggest writing prize, The Peggy Ramsay Award, for her play, *Refuge*; active in Scottish PEN's women writers committee and other groups, such as the SAC Scots Language Synergy and Cross Party Parliamentary Group for

the Scots Language; held three creative writing fellowships and received one of the first Creative Scotland Awards, plus a Canongate Prize and the Scots Language MacDiarmid Trophy; widely anthologised, her work includes six poetry collections including *Alien Crop* (Chapman, 1996 – shortlisted for the Scottish Book of the Year), *Reading the Bones* (Canongate, 1999), *Not for Glory* (2001), *Ye Cannae Win* (Chapman, 2002).

11 **JAMES T. R. RITCHIE** (1905–1998), was born in Edinburgh. The cover notes of *A Cinema of Days* indicate that many of its poems were written in the 1930s and that the poet read them on the radio, for which he also wrote plays and occasional talks. He also wrote film scripts – *The Grey Metropolis* and *The Flower and the Straw* – and a book on verse-writing by children, *The Gay Science*, and a book of short-stories, *The Ha'penny Millionaire*. He published two collections of Edinburgh school children's street songs – *The Singing Street* (1964) and *Golden City* (1965, both Oliver & Boyd, Edinburgh and London). He taught for over 30 years at Norton Park School and was a noted collector of Scottish Art.

12 **GEORGE GUNN** was born in Thurso in 1956, where he still lives; worked as a deep-sea fisherman, North Sea oil-driller, journalist; a playwright with some 20 professional productions, he is Artistic Director of Grey Coast Theatre Company which he co-founded in 1992; tutors in drama at North Highland College; newspaper and magazine essayist and reviewer; published a number of pamphlets and small collections, including for Chapman Publications *Sting* (1991), *Whins* (1996), *Winter Barley* (2005) and *Black Fish* (Scotia Review, 2004).

13 **ANGUS PETER CAMPBELL** was born on South Uist in 1950; educated at Edinburgh University and formerly worked as a lecturer, lobster-fisherman, forester, paper-radio-television journalist and columnist; in 2001 awarded the Bardic Crown for

Gaelic Poetry and a Creative Scotland Award; published six Gaelic novels and two collections of poetry – *The Greatest Gift* (1992) and *One Road* (1994); lives on the Isle of Skye with his wife and six children, where he holds the post of Iain Crichton Smith Writing Fellow with the Highland Council.

14   **BRIAN WHITTINGHAM** was born in Charing Cross, Glasgow, in 1950, and still lives there; left school at 15 years, worked in the Clyde shipyards, including building oilrigs and the QE2; a lecturer in Creative Writing at the Nautical College of Glasgow; was poetry editor for *West Coast* and *Nerve* magazines and writer-in-residence for East Lothian; awarded a fellowship to the Yaddo Artists Colony in New York in 1994; he is currently co-editor of New Writing Scotland; five poetry collections, including *Industrial Deafness* (Crazy Day Press, 1990), *Ergonomic Workstations & Spinning Tea Cans* (Taranis Books, 1992), *Swiss Watches & the Ballroom Dancer* (Taranis Books, 1996), *The Old Man From Brooklyn and the Charing Cross Carpet* (Mariscat Press, 2000), *Drink the Green Fairy* (Luath, 2004); a new collection from Luath Press, *Septimus Pitt and the Grumbleoids* (2007).

15   **ANGUS PETER CAMPBELL**, see note 13 for details.

16   **REV JOHN SKINNER** (1721–1807) was born at Balfour, Aberdeenshire, son of a schoolmaster. Educated at Marischal College, Aberdeen from the age of 13 years, becoming a schoolmaster at Kemnay, then at Monymusk. He became a minister in the Scottish Episcopal Church in 1742, remaining minister of Longside congregation until his death. The Episcopal clergy were severely clamped down following the 1745 Rebellion, and while no means a Stuart sympathiser, his chapel was burnt by Cumberland's troops and he was himself imprisoned between May–November 1753 for preaching to more than four persons through an open window, a practice still banned by the government. He pub-

lished a two-volume *Ecclesiastical History of Scotland* in 1788, and he was the author of several popular songs and poems.

17   GEORGE BRUCE was born in Fraserburgh (1909–2002); educated at Aberdeen University; a record producer for three decades with the BBC, latterly in Edinburgh; the landscape and the sea of the North-East permeate his early poems; anthologist and literary critic; *Today and Tomorrow, Collected Poems, 1939–2000* (2001) and the posthumous publication of *Through the Letterbox*, a selection of haikus to friends with illustrations by Elizabeth Blackadder (2003).

18   STEPHEN MULRINE was born in Glasgow in 1937. A former lecturer at Glasgow School of Art, he has also taught creative writing; his work ranges from poetry and short-stories to television and radio plays, serials and adaptations; since 1988 he has concentrated on translation, chiefly from Russian writers. See *Poems by Stephen Mulrine* (1971).

19   TOM MCGRATH was born in Rutherglen in 1940; an internationally known playwright and jazz pianist, he now lives in Kingskettle, Fife; in the mid-60s he was associated with the emerging UK underground culture, participating in Alexander Trocchi's *Project Sigma* and becoming founding editor of the *International Times*; in the 1970s worked with Billy Connelly on *The Great Northern Welly-Boot Show* and from 1974–77 he was director of the Third Eye Centre, an arts centre on Sauchiehall Street, Glasgow; in 1977 worked with Jimmy Boyle on his play *The Hardman*.

20   SYDNEY GOODSIR SMITH was born in New Zealand (1915–1975, Edinburgh) came to Edinburgh in his late teens to study medicine, which he failed in first year, then took history at Oriel College, Oxford; interest in medieval Scots led him to adopt

the language in most of his own work; wrote a rumbustious novel, *Carotid Cornucopius* (1947, 1964) and a verse drama, *The Wallace* (1960), and was an artist and cartoonist; wrote criticism and undertook editing, for example, with James Barke, *The Merry Muses of Caledonia* (1959); he was art critic for *The Scotsman* for several years, and died suddenly in 1975; *Collected Poems*, John Calder, 1975.

21   **EDWIN MORGAN** was born in Glasgow in 1920, and lived there all his life except when he was with the RAMC in the Middle East during the Second World War, and his poetry is grounded in the city; retired from Glasgow University as titular Professor of English in 1980 and served as Glasgow's first Poet Laureate 1999–2002, becoming in 2004 Scotland's first 'Scots Makar' – National Poet; his various awards include the Queen's Medal for Poetry (2000) and the prestigious Weidenfelf Prize for Translation (2001); endlessly prolific and inventive, eclectic and cosmopolitan, his output includes *Collected Poems* 1949–1987 (Carcanet, 1996), *Collected Translations* (1996), *New Selected poems* (2000), *Cathures* (2002), *A Book of Lives* (2007), and most recently, *Beyond the Sun* (Luath, 2007).

22   **DUNCAN GLEN** was born in Cambuslang in 1933; a management trainee and apprentice compositor in Glasgow and Kirkcaldy before gaining a scholarship to Edinburgh College of Art in 1954; after National Service worked in London as a freelance designer for publishers and a lecturer on design at the University of Lancashire and Nottingham Trent University, becoming the latter's Professor of Visual Communication in 1987; elected a Fellow of the Chartered Society of Designers in 1997 and received a Doctorate from Paisley University in 1998; wrote the first full critical study of MacDiarmid, *Hugh MacDiarmid and the Scottish Renaissance* (1964); edited *Akros Magazine* for 25 years, which placed Scottish literature in an international context; published

a number of anthologies and numerous collections of his own poetry, *Collected Poems:* 1965–2005 (2006).

23   **DOUGLAS DUNN** was born in Inchinnan, Renfrewshire in 1942; educated as a Librarian in Scotland then read English at the University of Hull, becoming a freelance writer in 1971; became Professor of English at St Andrew's University in 1991; member of the Scottish Arts Council 1992–94 and a Fellow of the Royal Society of Literature in 1981; won a Somerset Maugham Award, the Geoffrey Faber Memorial Prize, and has twice been awarded prizes by the Scottish Arts Council and the Hawthornden Prize for *St Kilda's Parliament* in 1981 and Whitbread Book of the Year Award for *Elegies* in 1985; written several radio and television plays, two collections of short stories and edited *The Faber Book of 20th-Century Scottish Poetry* (2000) and 10 poetry collections, including *The Donkey's Ears* (2000), *The Year's Afternoon* (2000) and *Selected Poems* 1964–2000 (2002).

24   **IAIN CRICHTON SMITH** was born in Glasgow (1928–1998, Taynuilt), brought up on the Island of Lewis from infancy; educated at Aberdeen University, spent most of his working life as a teacher in Clydebank then Oban, becoming a free-lance writer in 1977; wrote in prose and poetry and in English and Gaelic; wrote a classic novel about the Highland Clearances, *Consider the Lillies*, while the satirical 'Murdo' short stories appeared posthumously in 2001; published over 17 poetry collections – subsequent to his *Collected Poems* (Carcanet, 1995) were *The Leaf and the Marble* (1998) and *A Country for Old Men* (2000).

25   **WILLIAM NEILL** was born in 1922 in Prestwick, Ayrshire; educated in Celtic Studies and English at Edinburgh University and studied closely the poets of the Scottish Renaissance; writes in Scottish and Irish Gaelic, Lowland Scots and English; poetry awards include The Grierson Verse Prize (1970), Sloan Prize

(1970) and a Scottish Arts Council Book Award (1985); *Selected Poems, 1969–1992* (1994) and *Caledonian Cramboclink* (2001).

26   **PARRY MAGUIRE** was born in Liverpool in 1963, English graduate, John Moore's University, Liverpool and due to start teacher training in September 2007 and an MA in English at Salford University; now based in Rossendale, Lancashire; had her poems published over the years in various football and music related fanzines; proudest moment thus far has been having her poem *Just Fontaine* published in *Just Fontaine – Mes 13 Verites Sur Le Foot* ed Jean-Pierre Bonenfant; football heroes, Bill Shankly and Kenny Dalglish; her poems can be accessed on www.footballpoets.org.

27   **PARRY MAGUIRE**, see note 26 for details.

28   **ROBERT FERGUSSON** was born just off Edinburgh's Royal Mile, the son of Aberdeenshire parents. He studied at the University of St Andrews, where he began writing poetry and acquiring his flair for satire, but left without a degree after his father died. His early verse was in English, but his greatest works, full of vision, realism and wit, are chiefly in vivacious colloquial Scots. His short life was concluded by poor health and incarceration and he died aged just 24 in Edinburgh's Bedlam Mental Asylum. His grave went unmarked for 13 years until Robert Burns erected a monument in his name, commemorating him as 'my elder brother in misfortune, by far my elder brother in the muse'.

29   **ALAN BOLD** was born in Edinburgh (1943–1998), educated at Edinburgh University, graduating in 1965, the year of his first collection, *Society Inebrious*, four more following quickly with an appearance in 1970 in *Penguin Modern Poets* 15 plus the anthology, *The Penguin Book of Socialist Verse*, which seemed to

confirm his early mentoring by Hugh MacDiarmid, his critical biography of whom, *MacDiarmid,* won the McVitie's Prize as Scottish Writer of the Year in 1989; subsequent astounding literary output as a critic, commentator, editor and literary biographer, painter and poet – *In This Corner: Selected Poems 1963–1983* (Edinburgh, 1983) and *Illuminated Poems* (pictures combined with texts).

30   **NORMAN MacCAIG** was born in Edinburgh (1910–1996); studied classics at Edinburgh University and worked for many years as a primary school teacher; jailed as a conscientious objector during the Second World War; appointed Fellow in Creative Writing at Edinburgh in 1967 and became a Reader in Poetry at Stirling University in 1970; the landscape of Assynt was a recurrent theme; his work progressed from ingenious similes to 'a welcome sanity', according to Douglas Dunn, and he was a friend of Hugh MacDiarmid, not a follower – he called for 'two minutes pandemonium' at the great man's funeral; disowned his early books influenced by the New Apocalypse school and between *Riding Lights* (1955) to *Voice Over* (1988) he published 14 collections; *Collected Poems,* Chatto & Windus, London, 1988.

31   **CHRISTOPHER SALVESEN** was born in Edinburgh in 1935; after National Service he read English at Oxford University, pursuing an academic career at Trinity College Dublin and the University of Reading; published a study of Wordsworth, *The Landscape of Memory*; two poetry collections, *Floodsheaf, from a Parish History* (Whiteknights Press, 1974) and *Among the Goths* (Mercat Press, Glasgow, 1986).

32   **BILLY HUNTER** was one of the famous 'Ancell Babes', the Motherwell FC side which also included Ian St John and Pat Quinn; described by his manager, Bobby Ancell, as 'paradise to

watch', he was generally regarded as an 'elegant' inside-left (creative mid-fielder) who was capped three times for Scotland between 1960–61; the caption to his photo in Motherwell FC's official history calls him 'poetry in motion'; his own book of recollections, mostly in light-hearted verse, *Look Back in Amber and Claret* (1960s, copy in the Scottish Poetry Library) has a Foreword by Bob Crampsey.

33   **DONNY O'ROURKE** was born in Port Glasgow in 1959; educated at Glasgow University; worked in Arts television for several years as a film and programme maker before concentrating on writing, song-writing, performing and lecturing, including on Scottish Studies at the Glasgow School of Art; editor and anthologist, notably *Dream State* (Polygon, 1994, 2002) and *Ae fond Kiss: The Love Letters of Robert Burns and Clarinda* (Mercat, 2000); several poetry collections – including *The Waistband and other poems* (Polygon, 1997) and *On a Roll: a Jena Notebook* (Mariscat, 2001); received the Hermann Kesten Stipendium, and arising from his time in Nuremberg came the dual language collection *Aus dem Wartesaal der Poesie/From Poetry's Waiting Room* (Spatlese Verlag, Nurnberg, 2005); latest book is *The Lovely Word Republic* (2005).

34   **MATTHEW FITT** was born in Dundee in 1968; educated at Stirling University and worked as a teacher until he became a Brownsbank Fellow in 1995–97; travelled extensively and lived in Pribram in central Bohemia; a founding editor (with James Robertson) of Iṭchy Coo, a press for children's books in Scots; currently National Scots Language Development Officer; writes (and talks!) in Scots and English, his first novel in Scots, *But N Ben A-Go-Go* (2002) was published to critical acclaim by Luath, as was his second collection of poetry, *Kate O Shanter's Tale & other poems* (2003), also available on CD; first collection, *Pure Radge*, was published by Akros, 1996.

35   **WILLIAM HERSHAW** was born in Newport on Tay in 1957; edu-
cated at Edinburgh University and Craiglockhart College,
becoming an English teacher in 1980, now Principal Teacher
of English at Beath High School, Cowdenbeath; featured as
one of Donny O'Rourke's 'New Scottish Poets' in *Dream State*,
1994; first poems in Scots published in *Four Fife Poets* (1988),
The Cowdenbeath Man (1997) *Across the Water* (2000), *A Scots
Mass For Saint Andrae* (2001); in 2003 won the Callum
MacDonald Memorial Award for the pamphlet *Winter Song*;
Fifty Fife Sonnets – Coarse and Fine (Akros Publications,
Kirkcaldy, 2006); a musician and songwriter, he and his sisters
recorded a CD in 2004, *A Fish Laid at the Door*.

36   **GEORGE MACKAY BROWN** was born in Stromness, Orkney
(1921– 1996) the 'Hamnavoe' of his poems and stories; TB kept
him out of the forces in 1940; began writing for The Orkney
Herald and The New Shetlander; in 1951 and 1956 studied as
a mature student at Newbattle College under Edwin Muir,
then at Edinburgh University 1957–60; abandoned teacher
training and returned to Orkney in 1961; acclaimed novelist
and short-story writer, published 14 collections of poetry;
Collected Poems (2005) was published posthumously.

37   **ADRIAN MITCHELL** was born in London in 1932, father Scottish;
educated at Christ Church, Oxford; worked as a journalist
with the *Oxford Mail* and *Evening Standard*; a free-lance jour-
nalist and writer for adults and children since the mid-1960s
including poetry, novels, plays, and a libretti; an Eric Gregory
Award winner and Fellow of the Royal Society of Literature;
seven poetry collections, two for children – *For Beauty Douglas:
Adrian Mitchell's Collected Poems 1953–79* (1982), *Love Songs of
World War Three* (1983), *Greatest Hits: His 40 Golden Greats*
(1991), *Blue Coffee: Poems 1985–1996* (1996), *Heart on the
Left: Poems 1953–1984* (1997) and co-edited *Red Sky at Night:
An Anthology of British Socialist Poetry* (2003).

38 **RAYMOND VETTESE** was born in Arbroath in 1950, now lives in Montrose; worked as a journalist, barman, process worker, teacher of Scottish studies to Americans, and supply teacher; poems first published in *Four Scottish Poets* (1988); his first collection, *The Richt Noise and Ither Poems* (MacDonalds, Midlothian, 1988) won the Saltire Society's Scottish First Book Award in 1989, the same year he held the first William Soutar Writing Fellowship; President of the Scots Language Society, 1991–94; *A Keen New Air*, Saltire Society, (1995).

39 **MACFHIONGHAIN, CAILEIN/ COLIN MACKINNON** was born in Daliburgh, South Uist, in 1963, father a teacher, mother a nurse; educated at Edinburgh University; works as a TV reporter for BBC Scotland in Glasgow; published one other poem in 1999, 'Peacadh', in *Gairm 155, An Samhradh*, 1991 (originally printed in *Gairm 133* (*An Geamhradh* 1985–6).

40 **G. F. DUTTON**, an Anglo-Scottish poet and scientist; his mountaineering stories were collected in *The Complete Doctor Stories*; three of his books have won Scottish Arts Council Book Awards, and his last collection, *The Concrete Garden*, a Poetry Book Society Recommendation.

41 **LIZ LOCHHEAD** was born in Motherwell in 1947; trained at the Glasgow School of Art, became a teacher for several years; important dramatist, works in theatre and broadcasting; broke into the predominantly male domain of poetry with her first collection, *Memo for Spring* (1971), followed by *Dreaming Frankenstein and Collected Poems* (Polygon, 1984), *True Confessions and New Clichés* (Polygon, 1985), *Bagpipe Muzak* (Penguin, 1991) and *The Colour of Black & White: Poems 1984–2003* (Polygon, 2003); *Medea: an adaptation from Euripides* (Nick Hern Books, 2000 – won the Saltire Book of the Year Award, 2001); appointed Glasgow's Poet Laureate in 2005 in succession to Edwin Morgan.

42   **ALASTAIR MACKIE** was born in Aberdeen (1925–1995); studied at Aberdeen University; taught at Stromness Academy and Wade Academy, taking early retirement in 1983; awards from the Scottish Arts Council 1976, 1987; four collections of poetry, *Soundings* (Akros), *Clytach* (Akros), *Back-Green Odyssey* (Rainbow Books), *Ingaitherins: Selected Poems* (AUP, 1987).

43   **RON BUTLIN** was born in Edinburgh in 1949 and grew up in Dumfriesshire; educated at the University of Edinburgh; a freelance journalist with the *Sunday Herald* and the *TLS*; a poet, playwright novelist, short-story writer and opera librettist whose work has been translated into several languages; another collection of short-stories due in 2007, *No More Angels*; won a Scottish Arts Council Book Award for *Ragtime in Unfamiliar Bars* (1985); more recent collections: *Histories of Desire* (Bloodaxe,1995) and *Without a Backward Glance: new and selected poems* (2005).

44   **ALAN BOLD**, see note 29 for details

45   **WILLIAM MCILVANNEY** was born in Kilmarnock in 1936, son of a miner; educated at Glasgow University and worked as an English teacher between 1960–75; award winning novelist, acclaimed essayist, a fluent speaker and socialist-cultural commentator, published two collections of poems – *The Longships in Harbour: Poems* (Eyre & Spottiswoode, 1970) and *In Through the Head* (Mainstream, 1988).

46   **MACTHOMAIS, RUARAIDH/DERICK THOMSON** was born in Stornoway in 1921, lives in Glasgow; studied at Aberdeen and Cambridge Universities and became a University lecturer, becoming Professor of Celtic at the University of Glasgow 1963–91; Honorary President of the Scottish Poetry Library and a Fellow of the Royal Society of Edinburgh and the British Academy; co-founded and edited the Gaelic literary quarterly

magazine *Gairm* (1950–); an active Gaelic writer, scholar, critic and publisher, he compiled an *English-Gaelic* dictionary (1981) and *A Companion to Gaelic Poetry* (1983, 1994); published seven collections of Gaelic poetry with many English translations, including, *Plundering the Harp, Collected Poems 1940–1980* (MacDonalds, 1982) and *Meall Gargh/The Rugged Mountain* (Gairm Publications, 1995).

47 **DUNCAN GLEN**, see note 22 for details

48 **TOM LEONARD**, see note 5 for details.

49 **ALASTAIR MACKIE**, see note 42 for details.

50 **TOM LEONARD**, see note 5 for details.

51 **DENNIS O'DONNELL** was born in Bathgate in 1951; educated at Edinburgh University; principal teacher of English in West Lothian for several years; poetry critic for the Scots literary magazine *Cencrastus*; a columnist for *The Scotsman,* then took up psychiatric nursing; *Two Clocks Ticking* (Curly Snake Publishing, 1997) won a Saltire First Award from the Scottish Arts Council; second collection *Smoke and Mirrors* (Curly Snake Publishing, 2000); also a playwright and more recently has turned to writing short-stories and novels.

52 **PETE ST. JOHN** was born in Dublin; educated at Scoil Muire Gan Smal, Inchicore and Synge Street C.B.S.; an electrician, he emigrated to Canada, Alaska, Central America and the West Indies working as a professional athlete, truck driver, logging camp labourer, salesman and electrical contracting rep in the USA; deeply involved in the Peace and Civil Rights Movements before returning to Dublin in the 1970s, where he has become a successful singer-songwriter.

54   **ALISTAIR FINDLAY** was born in Winchburgh, West Lothian in 1949, trained as a social worker at Moray House, Edinburgh, and worked as a Local Authority social work manager until August 2007, when a Scottish Arts Council writer's bursary was awarded to complete a third collection of poems on social workers, *Dancing With Big Eunice*, and to edit an anthology on the Poetry of Scottish Marxism, *Lenin's Gramophone*; his social-cultural history of the shale-oil workers of West Lothian, *Shale Voices* (1999) was re-issued in 2007 by Luath Press, which also publishes his poetry collections, *Sex, Death and Football* (2003) and *The Love Songs of John Knox* (2006); he was a part-time provisional professional footballer with Hibernian FC between 1965–68.

55   **ROBERT CRAWFORD** was born in Bellshill, Lanarkshire in 1959; educated at Universities of Glasgow and Oxford, now Professor of Modern Scottish Literature at the University of St Andrews; prolific poet and literary critic; won an Eric Gregory Award in 1988, twice won a Scottish Arts Council Book Award, had four collections as Poetry Book Society Recommendations, is a Fellow of the Royal Society of Edinburgh, was a founder of *Verse* literary magazine in 1984 and poetry editor for Polygon in the 1990s, has co-edited two Penguin Anthologies of British, Irish and Scottish Verse; six collections of poetry – *A Scottish Assembly* (1990), *Talkies* (1992), *Masculinity* (1996), *Spirit Machines* (1999), *Tip of My Tongue* (2003), *Selected Poems* (2005) – and *Sharawaggi: Poems in Scots* (1990), with W. N. Herbert.

56   **ALASDAIR MacIVER** unable to provide further details.

57   **MIKE DILLON** was born in Cork in 1948 and raised from the age of eight in the Fenlands of Lincolnshire, moving to Edinburgh in

the mid-70s and becoming involved in the Writers Workshop movement; his poetry appeared in *New Writing Scotland* and *Lines Review* and many anthologies and magazines; twice winner of Edinburgh Folk Club's Song Competition, has performed his songs and poems in many clubs and festivals throughout Britain, Ireland, Germany, Austria, the Netherlands and the USA; lives in Newhaven, Edinburgh, and is currently working on a prose trilogy, the first volume of which, *Child From Water*, is due out next year; has published two solo poetry booklets, *Under the Rainbow* and *Red Herrings*.

58 **TOM LEONARD**, see note 5 for details.

59 **STEWART CONN** was born in Glasgow in 1936 and grew up in Ayrshire; lived in Edinburgh since 1977 and became its first poet laureate – Edinburgh Makar – between 2002–2005; drama producer for BBC Radio 1962–1992 and Head of Radio Scotland's drama department; numerous awards for poetry and has published plays and a memoir, *Distances* (Scottish Cultural Press, 2001); among many individual volumes are *Stolen Light: Selected Poems* (Bloodaxe, 1999) and *Ghosts at Cockcrow* (Bloodaxe, 2005); edited *100 Favourite Scottish Poems* (Luath Press & Scottish Poetry Library, 2006).

60 **JOHN MCCAUGHIE** was born in Edinburgh in 1958 and brought up in Cumnock, Ayrshire; works as a training officer with The Living Memory Association, a reminiscence project in Edinburgh; on returning to Edinburgh joined the Educational Association's writers workshop in 1979; published poems in various writers workshop publications and has performed poetry at the Edinburgh Fringe and Festivals at Newcastle, Hastings, Holland and Germany; a member of The Diggers Writers group, he is currently working on a novel.

61 **LEONARD S. QUINN** Unable to provide further details, although he seems to have been a familiar figure on the poetry scene in Glasgow in the late 1980s-early 1990s.

62 **TOM POW** was born in Edinburgh in 1950, now lives in Dumfries; currently Head of Creative and Cultural Studies at Glasgow University's Crichton Campus; has written radio drama, a travel book and picture books and novels for young people; was poet in residence at the 2002 Edinburgh Book Festival and at the StAnza Poetry Festival, 2005; four poetry collections, including *Landscapes and Legacies* (iynx, 2003) which was shortlisted for the Scottish Arts Council's Book of the Year Award.

63 **JAMES AITCHISON** was born in Stirlingshire in 1938 and educated at Glasgow and Strathclyde Universities; formerly a Senior Lecturer in Media Studies at Napier University; received an Eric Gregory award for poetry in 1968; five collections of poems published, most recently *Brain Scans* (1998), *Bird-Score* (2002) and a critical study, *The Golden Harvester: The Vision Of Edwin Muir* (1988); jointly-edited along with Alexander Scott the first three volumes of *New Writing Scotland;* other books, *Cassell's Dictionary of English Grammar* and *Writing for the Press: An Introduction*.

64 **MAURICE LINDSAY** was born in Glasgow in 1918; educated at the National Academy of Music, an injury to his wrist during the War prevented him becoming a musician; a broadcaster and music critic – with the late George Bruce edited and presented the BBC Radio Scotland programme 'Scottish Life and Letters'; some 20 volumes of poetry comprise *Collected Poems: 1940–1990* (Aberdeen); a prolific editor, critic and historian, his most notable books include *Modern Scottish Poetry: An Anthology of the Scottish Renaissance* 1920–1945 (Carcanet, revised 1966,

1976), *History of Scottish Literature* (London, 1977) and, with Lesley Duncan, *The Edinburgh Book of 20th Century Scottish Poetry* (Edinburgh University Press, 2005); first Director of the Scottish Civic Trust, and was nine years Honorary Secretary of Europa Nostra, the European conservation body; now lives with his wife in Bowling, Dunbartonshire.

65   **W. N. HERBERT** was born in Dundee in 1961; educated at Oxford University; Professor of Creative Writing at Newcastle University; co-founder with Richard Price in 1989 of *Gairfish*, the Scots Poetry Magazine; one of Penguin's New Generation Poets, several residencies and Writing Fellowships; critical study of MacDiarmid, *To Circumjack MacDiarmid* (OUP, 1992); short-listed for a number of prizes, including the Forward Poetry Prize (Best Collection), McVitie's Prize for Scottish Writer of the Year, T. S. Eliot Prize, Scottish Arts Council Book Awards for three of his collections, his more recent ones being published by Bloodaxe, *Forked Tongue* (1994), *Cabaret McGonagall* (1996), *The Lauderlude* (1998), *The Big Bumper Book of Troy* (2002), *Bad Shaman Blues* (2006, a Poetry Book Society Recommendation); edited various collections, anthologies and critical works including *Strong Words: Modern Poets on Modern Poetry* (2000); a vigorous cross-art projects collaborator.

66   **ROB PARAMAN** has had poems published by Flarestack, Australia, and moves around a lot, last heard of in Hove, East Sussex.

67   **JIM KAY** was born in Kilmarnock in 1930, became an electrician, then went to Glasgow University and was a teacher in Kilmarnock and Hamilton; published in various places, including *The New Makars,* ed Tom Hubbard; won third place in a joint Spectator/Johnny Walker Scots Poetry Competition 'a few years back'; now retired and lives in Prestwick; published one poetry collection, *A Bitia Tarzan Film* (1987).

68   **ALISTAIR FINDLAY**, see note 54 for details.

69   **HUGH MCMILLAN** was born in 1955, a history teacher in Dumfries; won the Scottish National Poetry Competition in 1984; awarded Scottish Arts Council writer's bursaries in 1988, 1991 and 1993; also a short-story writer; poetry collections include *Tramontana* (1990), *Horridge* (1994) and *Aphrodite's Anorak* (1996).

70   **ROBERT ALAN JAMIESON** was born in Sandness, Shetland in 1958; abandoned the security of an oil-company salary to write two novels and a collection of poetry, *Shoormal*, in the 1980s, then studied literature at Edinburgh University from 1988 as a mature student, publishing a third novel in 1991; William Soutar Fellowship in Perth, 1993–96; co-edited *Edinburgh Review*, 1993–98; Creative Writing Fellow at the Universities of Glasgow and Strathclyde, 1998–2001; featured as one of Donny O'Rourke's 'New Scottish Poets' in *Dream State*, 1994, his poems appear in many anthologies; a playwright and inveterate cross-arts collaborator, recent publications, with the painter Graeme Todd, *Mount Hiddenabyss* (Fruitmarket Gallery, 2000), and *Ansin T'Sjaetlin: some responses to the language question* (Samisdat, 2005).

71   **MIKE HARDING** was born in Manchester in 1944 into a working-class Irish-Catholic family. His father was killed returning from a bombing mission four weeks before Mike was born. He was encouraged to write by his English teacher, Father 'Foxy' Reynolds, at St Bede's School. Music led him into the pub and Folk Club circuit, and he left teaching to become a full-time entertainer in 1967. In 1975 the record 'The Rochdale Cowboy' put him into the mainstream. He has published three poetry collections – *The Singing Street* (Moonraker, 1979), *Daddy Edgar's pools* (Peterloo Poets, 1992), *Crystal Set Dreams* (Peterloo Poets, 1997).

72 **LORNA J. WAITE** was born and brought up in Kilbirnie, Ayrshire and educated at Garnock Academy. She has an MA in Psychology and MSC in Community Education from Edinburgh University. She has written on the arts for a variety of publications and artists; *The Scotsman, List, Portfolio, Edinburgh Review, Variant* and worked as West Lothian Arts Co-ordinator for Artlink. Currently doing a practise-based PhD at the Visual Research Centre, University of Dundee. Received a Wingate Scholarship for work on steel industry in Ayrshire which led to PhD and New Writers Bursary from Scottish Arts Council. She is a Gaelic Learner.

73 **ANDREW GREIG** was born in Bannockburn in 1951, grew up in Anstruther, Fife; educated at Edinburgh University; a former Glasgow University Writing Fellow and Scottish Arts Council Scottish/Canadian Exchange Fellow; an acclaimed novelist and poet, he lives in Orkney and the Borders; published five novels, including *In Another Light* (Saltire Society Book of the Year, 2004), and six collections of poetry, the last being *Into You* (Bloodaxe, 2001) and *This Life, This Life: Selected Poems 1970–2006*, (Bloodaxe, 2006), two books chronicling his Himalayan expeditions and a memoir, *Preferred Lies* (Weidenfeld & Nicolson, 2006).

74 **JACKIE KAY** was born in Edinburgh in 1961 to a Scottish mother and Nigerian father; adopted at birth by a white Scottish couple and brought up in Glasgow; her adoptive father was Scottish Organiser for the Communist Party of Great Britain; she lives in Manchester with her son Matthew; studied at the Royal Scottish Academy of Music and Drama and read English at Stirling University; a fellow of The Royal Society of Literature and Lead Advisor to the Literature Department at the Arts Council of Great Britain; teaches creative writing at Newcastle University, four collections of poetry, all published by Bloodaxe,

The Adoption Papers (1991 – winner of a Forward Prize, a Saltire Prize, and a Scottish Arts Council Book Award), *Other Lovers* (1993 – won the Somerset Maugham Award), *Off Colour* (1998 – shortlisted for the 1999 T. S. Eliot Award), *Life Mask* (2005); an award winning novelist, short-story writer, she has written for stage, television and radio and worked with the composer Mark Anthony Turnage.

75   **LILIAN ANDERSON** was born in Glasgow in 1945; left school at 15 and went to work in John Menzies warehouse, surrounded by books! Published in various magazines over the years, including *Markings* and *Northwords* and some English ones; one poetry collection, *Stanes and Leaves*.

76   **ANONYMOUS**

77   **ANGUS CALDER** was born in Surrey in 1942; best known as a historian, journalist, academic and critic, he began writing poetry regularly in his 50s; won an Eric Gregory Award in 1967; Staff Tutor for the Open University in Scotland and Convener of the Scottish Poetry Library on its founding in 1984; held academic posts in New Zealand and Zimbabwe and a prolific author, editor and essayist; has lived in Edinburgh for the last 20 years and has several collections of poetry published – *Waking in Waikato* (Diehard, 1997), *Colours of Grief* (Shoestring Press, 2002), *Dipa's Bowl* (Aark Arts, 2004), *sun behind the castle* (Luath, 2004).

78   **SARAH WARDLE** was born in London in 1969; studied classics at Oxford University and English at Sussex University; a lecturer at Middlesex University, she was Poet in Residence for Tottenham Hotspur FC; essayist and reviewer for *Poetry Review, Times Higher Education Supplement, Times Literary Supplement, The Observer*; won the Geoffrey Dearmer Memorial

Prize in 1999 and was shortlisted for the Forward Poetry Prize (Best First Collection) for *Fields Away* (Bloodaxe, 2003); also *Score!* (Bloodaxe, 2005).

79   **D. M. BLACK** was born in South Africa in 1941, the son of a Scottish academic, raised in Malawi and Tanzania, moved to Scotland 1950; educated at Edinburgh University and taught at Chelsea Art College, took a post-grad degree in Religion at Lancaster University then trained as a psychotherapist; his translations of Goethe have been published in Modern Poetry in Translation, Poetry London and Chapman; collections include *With Decorum* (1967), *The Educators* (1969), *The Happy Crow* (1974), *Gravitations* (1979), *Collected Poems* (1991).

80   **ROBERT GARIOCH** was born and died in Edinburgh (1909–1981); educated at Edinburgh University in the 1930s where he met Sorley MacLean – poems by both appeared in *17 Poems for 6d*, published in 1940 by Chalmers Press (ie Garioch); a prisoner of war for most of its duration in Italy and Germany; worked as a teacher in the London area before and after the war, returning to Edinburgh in the late 1950s as a teacher until early retirement in the mid 1960s; later worked at the School of Scottish Studies and was Edinburgh University's Writing Fellow 1971–73; *Selected Poems* (1966) and *Collected Poems* (1977) both published by MacDonald.

81   **RAYMOND VETTESE**, see note 38 for details.

82   **BASHABI FRASER** was born in West Bengal and after a London childhood returned to India and attended a convent boarding school in the Himalayas, then university education in Bengal at Presidency College, then Lady Brabourne College to which her parents transferred her as they feared she might be imprisoned or worse through her involvement in radical student

politics; Honours and Masters Degrees in English Literature and a PhD from Edinburgh University; works as a lecturer for the Open University and is a Post-doctoral Fellow at the Centre for South Asian Studies at Edinburgh University; has written children's stories, a puppet play and co-edited two anthologies, *Edinburgh, An Intimate City* (Edinburgh Council, 2000), *Rainbow World* (2003), and three collections, *Life* (Diehard, 1997), *With Best Wishes from Edinburgh* (Calcutta, 2003), *tartan & turban* (Luath, 2004).

83 **JULIA DARLING** was born in Winchester in 1956 (died of cancer, 2005, Newcastle, where she had been resident since 1980); educated at Falmouth School of Art and worked as a community arts worker until she began writing full-time in 1987, when her first novel was longlisted for the Orange Prize; her last novel was longlisted for the Man Booker Prize and in 2003 she won the Northern Rock Foundation Award; she was diagnosed with cancer aged 38 and she wrote a collection of poetry about her experience of it, *Sudden Collapses in Public Places*, and a play, *Eating the Elephant* (1998), was nominated for three awards. She is survived by two daughters and claimed Scottish ancestry in her poem, *Ancestry*.

84 **KEN MORRICE** was born in Aberdeen (1924–2002), native Aberdonian and a medical graduate of Aberdeen University, a psychiatrist; several volumes published, one gaining a Scottish Arts Council Book Award; occasionally wrote short-stories; poetry collections include *The Scampering Marmoset* (1990), *Selected Poems* (1991), *Talking of Michelangelo* (1996).

85 **JOHN BURNSIDE** was born in Dunfermline in 1959 and lives in East Fife; a Reader in Creative Writing at the University of St Andrews; five novels and a recently acclaimed memoir, *A Lie About My Father* (2006); 10 collections of poetry published

including *The Myth of the Twin* (1994), *The Asylum Dance* (2000 – which won The Whitbread Poetry Award), *The Light Trap* (2002), *The Good Neighbour* (2005) and *Selected Poems* (2006); latest collection *Gift Song* (2007).

86 **TOM BRYAN** was born in Manitoba, Canada in 1950, and a long-term resident Scot; worked at various jobs, steeplejack, salmon farmer, now Arts Development Officer in Caithness; was an Aberdeenshire writing fellow 1994–97; edited the literary magazine *Northwords* 1992–97; married with two children, lives in Strathkinaird, Wester Ross; three collections of poems, *North East Passage* (1996), *Wolfwind* (Chapman, Edinburgh, 1996), *Wolfclaw Chronicles* (2000).

87 **SEAN O'BRIEN** was born in London in 1952 and grew up in Hull; educated at Cambridge and studied as a postgraduate at the universities of Birmingham, Hull and Leeds; school teacher between 1981–1989; a fellow in creative writing at Dundee University 1989–1990; co-founded the literary magazine *The Printer's Devil* and a regular reviewer for the *Sunday Times* and *Times Literary Supplement*, radio broadcaster and literary critic; numerous prizes and awards including an Eric Gregory Award, 1979, Somerset Maugham Award (1984, for *The Indoor Park*, Bloodaxe, 1983), two Forward Poetry Prizes, in 1995 for *Ghost Train* (Oxford University Press) and in 2001 for *Downriver* (Picador); recently turned to drama and musical writing; two books of literary criticism, *The Deregulated Muse* (1998) and *The Firebox* (1998).

88 **ALISTAIR FINDLAY**, see note 54 for details.

89 **STEPHEN SCOBIE** was born in Carnoustie in 1943, emigrated to Canada aged 21; began publishing poetry in the mid-60s; teaches at the University of Victoria; a literary critic influenced

by Jacques Derrida he has wide ranging interests including Bob Dylan, Leonard Cohen, cubism, concrete poetry, text and sound poetry; established with Shirley Neuman and Douglas Barbour the Longspoon Press in the early 1980s; received the Governor General's Award for Poetry in 1980 with *McAlmon's Chinese Opera* (Dunvegan, Ontario, Quadrant Editions) and elected to the Royal Society of Canada in 1995.

90 **ANONYMOUS** *c.* 1650

91 **TOM LEONARD**, see note 5 for details.

92 **ANDREW MCGEEVER** was brought up in Fife, studied at Edinburgh University and has taught maths for 33 years at Portobello High School. His poems have been hung in the National Museum of Scotland, exhibited in the Brooklyn Botanic Garden, New York, and carved in granite beside the 51st Highland Division memorial statue in Perth. He has been published in Canada by the Victoria Writers Society, *The Herald* newspaper and in the official magazines of both Celtic and Rangers Football Clubs. His poems have appeared in several magazines and he has read at the Edinburgh Festival Fringe and recently for the Shore Poets. He has won diplomas in the Scottish International Poetry Competition. He says that writing poetry keeps him sane, and that his friends agree.

93 **JOHN MCGILVRAY** unable to provide further details

94 **DON PATERSON** was born in Dundee in 1963; pursued a career in music, living in London and Brighton, returning in 1993 as Writer in Residence at Dundee University until 1996 when he became poetry editor at Picador; lives in Kirriemuir, Angus and continues as a musician, editor and writer; innumerable awards and prizes – won best first collection Forward Prize for *Nil Nil*

(Faber, 1993), while *God's Gift to Women* (Faber, 1997) won both the Geoffrey Faber Memorial Prize and the TS Eliot Prize for Poetry, the latter of which he won again, the only poet to do so, for *Landing Light* (Faber, 2004) which also won the Whitbread Prize for Poetry; other collections include *The Eyes* (Faber, 1999).

95   **PARRY MAGUIRE**, see note 26 for details.

96   **IAN MCMILLAN** was born in Darfield, South Yorkshire in 1956; educated at North Staffordshire Polytechnic; a poet, broadcaster, commentator and radio/TV programme-maker for over 20 years; founded a performance poetry group called Versewagon/ Circus of Poets; amongst other residences/fellowships, he has been Poet in Residence for Barnsley Football Club and for Humberside Police Force; he has written poetry for children and his collections for adults include *Dad, the Donkey's on Fire* (Carcanet, 1994), *I Found this Shirt* (Carcanet, 1998) and *Perfect Catch* (Carcanet, 2000): his website is www.ian-mcmillan.co.uk

97   **PARRY MAGUIRE**, see note 26 for details.

98   **IAN STEPHEN** was born in Stornoway in 1955 and still lives on Lewis, former lighthouse keeper; published in periodicals in many countries since 1979; received a Creative Scotland Award, contributed to Zenomap (Venice Biennale 2003) and represented Scotland at 'Poetry without Borders' in the Czech Republic, 2004; with artist Pat Law and musician Norman Chalmers produced in 2006 an exhibition of paintings, sculpture and sound about a group of islands called the Shiants; several poetry collections, including *Malin, Hebrides, Minches* (Dangaroo Press, Denmark, 1983), *Varying States of Grace* (Polygon, 1989), *Mackerel & Cremola* (pocketbooks, 2001) and *It's about this* (Nomad/Survivors Press, 2004).

99 **ALISTAIR FINDLAY**, see note 54 for details.

100 **JAMES ROBERTSON** was born in Kent in 1958, lived in Scotland from the age of six; he runs the pamphlet imprint Kettillonia and lives in Newtyle, Angus; a poet, editor, short-story writer and prize-winning novelist, he is general editor of Itchy Coo, the Scots language imprint for schools and young people; one book-length collection, *Sound Shadow* (B&W Publishing, 1995), and various pamphlets including *I Dream of Alfred Hitchcock* (Kettillonia, 1999) and *Stirling Sonnets* (2001), and *Voyage of Intent: Sonnets and Essays from the Scottish Parliament* (Scottish Book Trust/Luath Press, 2005) the result of being for three days the first writer in residence at the Scottish Parliament in November 2004.

INDEX OF POETS